RESEARCH CONVERSATIONS AND NARRATIVE

RESEARCH CONVERSATIONS AND NARRATIVE

A Critical Hermeneutic Orientation in Participatory Inquiry

Ellen A. Herda

Westport, Connecticut
London

Library of Congress Cataloging-in-Publication Data

Herda, Ellen A., 1940–
    Research conversations and narrative : a critical hermeneutic
orientation in participatory inquiry / Ellen A. Herda
        p.   cm.
    Includes bibliographical references and index.
    ISBN 0–275–96105–2 (alk. paper)
    1. Social sciences—Research. 2. Group problem solving.
3. Organization. I. Title.
H62.H424   1999
300'.72—dc21   98–53396

British Library Cataloguing in Publication Data is available.

Library of Congress Catalog Card Number: 98–53396
ISBN: 0–275–96105–2

First published in 1999

Praeger Publishers, 88 Post Road West, Westport, CT 06881
An imprint of Greenwood Publishing Group, Inc.
www.praeger.com

Printed in the United States of America

The paper used in this book complies with the
Permanent Paper Standard issued by the National
Information Standards Organization (Z39.48–1984).

10 9 8 7 6 5 4 3 2 1

To the memory of my mother
Alta I. Bestul Herda

Contents

Acknowledgments

I thank

the University of San Francisco in the person of its deans of the School of Education, particularly Paul Warren, for the opportunity to teach, especially my research courses, from a critical hermeneutic perspective to professionals from all walks of life and for the funding support and release time to write this book;

my many students who have been my coworkers in the creation of the inquiry protocol presented in this book, particularly M. Celeste Gonzales, Carolyn Nelson, Jo Williams, and Craig Zachlod for their willingness to share excerpts and adaptations from their own doctoral research and Mary Abascal-Hildebrand for analysis of her conversation with Issariyaporn Chulajarta and for her continued friendship and colleagueship in research, writing, and teaching;

my former students who now work in the fields of industry, health, education, government, and community development in many nations and who bring into the worlds of work a new concept of being, identity, and practice;

my former students, now colleagues, who teach with me that the world in front of the text can signify a just institution — Dave Ancel, Susan Bethanis, LeAnn McGinely, Larry Johnson, and Richard Culp Robinson;

my current doctoral students, Kelly Carey, Nancy Fitzmaurice, George Guim, Nathan Johnson, Paulette Powell, and Debra Sheldon, and master's student, Andrew Brown, whose research in adult and distant learning, pedagogy, health, and organization and community development will create new texts for appropriation and fusion of horizons in the everyday work lives of many people;

my future students;

Richard J. Bernstein whose enthusiasm during a meeting at California State University at Hayward in 1986 greatly encouraged me to continue to develop a research program in the tradition of critical hermeneutics for applied fields of endeavor including education, business and health and for introducing me to Paul Ricoeur;

Paul Ricoeur for coming to the University of San Francisco in 1987 to present a draft of his work on personal identity and narrative and for his presence and supportive nature to my students and me that were significant in shaping the research and practice of several generations of students who now weave teachings and research in critical hermeneutics into their lives;

Robert Bellah, Katherine Blamey, C. A. Bowers, Hubert Dreyfus, Elliot Eisner, Fernando Flores, William Langan, William Sullivan, Terry Winograd, and many others whose significant insights and remarks contributed to the inroads made that more firmly set in place the direction of critical hermeneutic research at the University of San Francisco School of Education, especially Robert Bellah (for his response to Paul Ricoeur's address) and C. A. Bowers (for his response to Terry Winograd's address and for his teachings on language and culture to me and to my doctoral student;

Bracha Klein and Linda Clark for helping to organize the Critical Hermeneutics Conference and for continuing in their professional lives the creation and recognition of social texts for their own students;

John R. Devine and Mary Celeste Rouleau, S.M.;

Richard Chaney (1940–97) for his teaching, encouragement, and enthusiasm; and

my family, especially Everett and Vicky.

Introduction:
The Social and Communicative
Nature of Research

Participatory research[1] in a critical hermeneutic tradition invokes language, understanding, and action. The nature of language, the responsibility for understanding, and the meaning of action are issues of increasing concern for social science researchers. In education, business, health, and government institutions we see an intensifying need to approach problems collaboratively that moves beyond negotiations or coercive policies, intervention or implementation of a new program, or the latest technique. More importantly, we need to acknowledge and understand that humans have the capacity to live in community and to address and solve problems together in organizations and social settings. Successful personal relationships in our lives are of significant importance. However, we also need to develop ways in which we live out meaningful lives in our organizational institutions. Ricoeur (1992: 194) recognizes that the good life is not only a personal matter but also an institutional matter. He describes that "living well is not limited to interpersonal relations but extends to the life of institutions," whereas institution is characterized by "the bond of common mores and not that of constraining rules." This book addresses how social scientists can work together with others to bring to life, in a practical and just manner, a process for critiquing existing social realities and creating new ones. Briefly and simply stated, this process entails a redescription or refiguration of our existing worlds in our organizations and communities.

The work of participatory research is a text created by the researcher and the research participants that opens the possibility of movement from text to action. The text refigures the world under consideration and, in so doing, engenders new possible worlds in the shared meanings obtained among the members through the research act. As Ricoeur (1995: 283) points out, "the refiguration of the world by the text does not occur unless it becomes a 'shared meaning'." The redescription or refiguration emerges with others through critique, genuine conversation, and imagination. All of these can ultimately result in confrontation, fragmentation, and fear unless there is an orientation to reach understanding and a willingness to assume responsibility to work with others to change current conditions. The creation of a text is a collaborative achievement, and by virtue of people working together to uncover shared meanings there is opened in front of the text the possibility of a different and presumably better world. This world is not validated by scientific criteria that measure neutrality, simplicity, or repeatability.

The world we propose through participatory research finds its legitimacy in our organizations and communities — in our language, understanding, and action. Ricoeur (1995: 283) reasons that the "presumed truth of the redescription of the world can, therefore, only be intersubjective." This intersubjectivity becomes the domain that eventually allows the world of the text to be complemented by the life-world of the teacher, the chief executive officer, or the researcher. If the world of the text is not complemented by the life-world of the members of the research population, the research is incomplete. This idea is drawn from the same parallel Ricoeur (1985: 160) uses in his investigation of the problems of a literary work — the complementarity of the world of the text and the life-world of the reader.

When we work together in a spirit of critique, understanding, and shared responsibility, we can appropriate a specified future. Such a future seems to call into consideration two primary points: understanding ourselves in communal life and changing the social and political relationships among various sectors and members of our organizations and society, including the relationship between researcher and members of the research population. Researchers have the responsibility to reflect critically upon their philosophy of research. Ultimately, such reflection may change one's research paradigm and cause a concomitant change in methodologies. Today, more than ever in the face of social and political challenges, researchers need to heed moral imperatives about how they collect data; how they interpret and use data; and how they, as researchers and members of social and organizational communities, need to act.

There are two related reasons why this type of research agenda is not an easy task. The first has to do with the theoretical background of most researchers, and the second has to do with community. The background predominantly is the positivist paradigm in which researchers attempt to formulate a neutral or unbiased methodological stance to carry out either quantitative or qualitative research. Often there is the mistaken understanding that if one does qualitative research this choice provides a substantive option to quantitative research. However, most often only techniques are changed. The research paradigm is still grounded in an epistemological and positivist framework. Within such an epistemological paradigm the researcher, although perhaps passionately caring about the issue at hand, is still removed methodologically from the problem and merely serves as a collector and analyzer of data. This is not to say that collecting and analyzing data never have a useful purpose. We need to organize data, for example, into explanations and sequence to determine the best course of action. However, these intellectual and technical enterprises do not yield understandings or lead to ontologically changed selves in relationship to others. We need to recognize that explanations are subsumed under interpretations and understandings and are of a lesser order in studying our social settings. Explanations cannot serve as a basis for judgments because they do not contain moral imperatives, as do interpretations.

[margin note: researchers are stuck in a positivistic paradigm]

The interpretative research agenda is not an easy task because more researchers and the research population are not aware of a need for community, springing from the research process, that engenders commitment and support to move social science inquiry beyond intellectual, technical enterprises to more philosophical and practical projects.

[margin note: need for community to support research and move it beyond research]

This book addresses both issues. It offers a theoretical framework for carrying out research in a critical hermeneutic tradition. Hermeneutic means interpretation; thus, critical hermeneutics, in a general sense, means passing judgment on that interpretation—speaking out on its legitimacy. Until Heidegger, hermeneutic simply meant interpretive analysis. After Heidegger, it took different turns, such as analytical, philosophical, or critical hermeneutics. In this text, hermeneutics after Heidegger refers to the critical turn, primarily fashioned by Paul Ricoeur and grounded in philosophical hermeneutics of Gadamer and critical theory of Habermas. Accordingly, this book presents practical examples of participatory research projects based in a critical hermeneutic tradition where researchers and research participants worked collaboratively on the problem, including data gathering, and a determination of meaning and significance of the issues at hand. The examples encompass education, business, policy, and international development in various cultural contexts, including the United States, the Philippines, Thailand, and Nepal. The common denominator of these research projects is the lessons on how we, in our organizations and communities, can further understand ourselves and our challenges from what we learn from each other at home and abroad. This is not to say that other countries necessarily have the answer for how we should educate adults, for example, or how we should do business. Rather, it is a means for placing ourselves in perspective, for seeing ourselves differently whether we are researchers, teachers, or engineers. Most importantly, it is a means for learning how to think about problems in a different light.

We are always in a historical situation without fully knowing how our history and language influence us. It is with humility that we should come to any understanding about ourselves — in view of the disparate and traumatic conditions of society, education, and health provision — and look with a critical eye on our claims to social science knowledge. To uncover how our history affects us we can look at language and tradition. The language we speak holds our history, and an investigation into our language reveals a story that we could never hear simply by being a participant-observer or by having people fill out a survey. Survey research or participant observation does not serve us in the study of many types of problems, especially those that call for new understanding. A record or text of a participant-observer influenced by a functionalist approach and a participant in a conversation in a hermeneutic tradition yield vastly different data. Yet, we have relied on rationalistic approaches virtually to the exclusion of interpretive research frameworks.

In the process of participatory research we end with a narrative. This narrative has the power to hold several plots, even those that may be contradictory. What is the identity of such a narrative? Ricoeur (1988: 248) describes the narrative identity as "not a stable and seamless identity." He further states that just as narrative identity gives us the possibility "to compose several plots on the subject of the same incidents (which, then, should not really be called the same events), so it is always possible to weave different, even opposed, plots about our lives." Participatory research can chronicle the events, goals, means, people, and consequences of our lives. It can also develop a story as a whole that opens up new ways of thinking and acting, which may appear contradictory but which in actuality provide a new sense of time and order of importance of our activities.

To gain a subtler understanding of the contrast between traditional and interpretive research, we can look at Aristotle's distinction between

techne and *phronesis*. In the performance of traditional positivist or functionalist research, we learn how to use specific techniques; in other words,
we gain skills. Technical expertise, or *techne*, is learned but can be forgotten. However, ethical knowledge, or *phronesis*, is moral judgment and
can be neither learned nor forgotten. Actions in our communities, organizations, and schools have moral implications. We do not act in situations
void of consequences. In all aspects of our lives, we are by implication
obliged to use moral knowledge and apply it in particular situations.

Techne and *phronesis* are types of knowledge. In our use of moral judgment (*phronesis*), we do not judge as one individual apart from others; we
do not apply a pre-given universal strategy to a particular situation as we
do in statistical research. Rather, a moral act involves another person as
we undergo a particular situation together, including research, where we
make a judgment that mediates between universal ideas and particular
contexts. The application of statistical techniques to data is a different act
than mediating moral principles that are inherent in our forms of rationality to specific social texts. Gadamer claims that *phronesis* characterizes all
authentic understanding.

What we see, how we act, and how we reason all determine the extent
and limit of our understanding. Gadamer (1988: 269) uses the image of a
horizon to express the limitations and potentials of our understanding. He
writes, "the horizon is the range of vision that includes everything that can
be seen from a particular vantage point. . . . A person who has no horizon
is a man who does not see far enough and hence overvalues what is nearest to him."[2] Gadamer continues to explain that when our horizons change
our understanding changes. Although our horizons are open, they are also
finite. It is up to us to change our horizons — the burden for understanding is on each of us.

Research is a reflective and communal act. As Kraeder (1974:
342–343) points out: "The study of man is at the same time man's act
upon himself as subject and object; it is a mode of human labor that is the
precondition and the consequence of every other." This is the case
because in social science research the interpretive nature of language
allows for new understanding, evaluation, and action, and the researcher
is always engaged in the act of research. The researcher does not generate
neutral data.

Often problems a researcher studies in a participatory mode are common to both the researcher and the participants. However, if there is not a
shared problem, through the research process both researcher and participants have the opportunity to learn. Research is a shared process of understanding and possible action with those in the research population as well

as a vehicle by which we can recognize our potential and our mistakes. Further, it is an ongoing act, like culture, that is always in the making. Brown (1985: 71) writes about participatory research in the following way: "Participatory research can change the understanding of both outside researchers and local participants as well as catalyze shifts in activity by all parties. Potentially, participatory research can produce mutual education, new knowledge, and solutions for specific problems." Even more important than new knowledge and solutions are the new understandings that can take place among people working together.

EFFECTS OF PARTICIPATORY RESEARCH

In applied critical hermeneutic research there needs to be an orientation to reach understanding among the participant(s) and researcher. Here, objectivity, sought by establishing an intersubjective or common understanding of the problem and possible alternatives carried out in the real world, is distinguished from neutrality that characterizes research in the positivist tradition. In social sciences, the idea of generating neutral data is naive. The validity of a research project using a participatory research mode resides in the work that follows the research project itself. Whether it is valid is a question that needs to be addressed by the people facing the problems under consideration. Mishler (1990) takes a somewhat different view of validation in his work. He distinguishes this concept from adherence to formalized rules. He suggests that validation has to do with trustworthiness and that validity claims are tested through ongoing discourse among researchers. I think the testing in discourse is part of validation, but, from my experience, I believe that a more final, though not necessarily ultimate, validity rests in the ways personal, social, and organizational relationships change among people.

I began the participatory research program at the University of San Francisco in 1981. To educate people to perform research in a hermeneutic tradition demands time and commitment on the part of both the teacher and student. The time does not take shape so much in hours, days, weeks, or months but rather in a refiguration of who we are as educators and researchers. This process is an evaluative one where our traditions are set before us in a critical mode and in our visions for the future. A fusion of our research horizon comes in rethinking the nature of language to include moral and political imperatives.

HER BACKGROUND & INFLUENCES

From a historical perspective, participatory research, developed from an educative process envisioned and used by Paulo Freire and further elaborated upon by Budd L. Hall and Bonnie Cain, set an important stage for collaborative research in non-industrialized countries. Although from a different tradition, Paulo Freire and Budd Hall helped me to define my own research process. Charles Keiffer's (1981) presentation at a session I organized at the Applied Anthropology meetings in Edinburgh, Scotland, further influenced my research protocol, especially in the exchange of the conversation text between the researcher and participants. Paul Ricoeur's work on text, time, and narrative identity has had the most profound influence on my work on participatory research. When he visited the University of San Francisco in May 1987 at the conference I organized on Critical Understandings for Critical Times, Professor Ricoeur spoke on the work that eventually was published in *Oneself as Another*. The conversations at this conference further shaped the ontology of participatory research in the critical hermeneutic tradition invoking the potential of humans to reflect on their history and to imagine worlds we could inhabit.

[margin handwriting: HX BKGR AND INFLU]

Freire, Hall, and Cain work within a Marxist and critical pedagogy tradition. Keiffer is influenced by the phenomenological and psychological traditions of researchers, such as Colaizzi and Giorgi. The writings and research in this book follow the basic tenets of critical hermeneutics, influenced by Ricoeur, Habermas, and Gadamer, as well as others. Although there are significant differences among the critical pedagogical, phenomenological, and hermeneutic approaches to participatory research, there is an important overlap. A common denominator among these various philosophical frameworks is the recognition that language is a critical medium for any meaningful social change to take place. Critical hermeneutics places the locus of both social and personal change in language and in tradition. An essential point in critical hermeneutic participatory research is that it is in language and our tradition that we have our very being. This ontological imperative positions both researcher and participants to view problems from different perspectives within a framework from which individuals see themselves as having personal and civic responsibilities over personal and social rights. Further, the identity of an individual does not arise from a developmental process resulting in a separate unit that when united with many others makes up a group, society, or community. Rather, the identity of an individual is found in a moral relationship with others which, when in aggregate form, makes up more than the sum of the membership. A full and mature sense of self does not stem from a developmental process grounded in individualism but instead arises from a recognition that in one's relationship with others there resides the possibility of seeing and understanding the world, and therefore one's self, differently. When I change, the rest of the world changes.

[margin handwriting: LANG. IS KEY FOR SOCIAL CHANGE TO HAPPEN]

[margin handwriting: INDIVIDUALITY FROM COMM. & RELATIONSHIPS]

For several decades in the United States, as well as in other countries, much effort has been expended on behalf of millions of people who are not in a position to exercise their personal and social rights. Most of these people still need, perhaps more than ever, advocates to work on behalf of the rights they ought to have but do not have. However, most of us need to exercise our sense of responsibility more than our rights in order to change and improve society. This begins with a sense of who we are and what our responsibilities are, wherever we find ourselves, whether in a just or in an unjust system.

Many of the arguments in this book will find resonance with various schools of thought that are critical of the structuralist and analytical philosophies. For example, research methodologies influenced by phenomenology, symbolic interaction, and critical ethnography may identify with the strong reliance in this work on social interaction, interpretation, and reflection as integral processes to appropriating new worlds in which our actions may take place.

Additionally, critical social scientists, particularly critical pedagogical writers, will see common ground between critical pedagogy and critical hermeneutic participatory research in that at the heart of both agendas are the following convictions: work to change organizations and society to embody more responsive and inclusive communities; reject the emphasis on scientific predictability based on the assumption that it is possible to norm human beings; question and change the legitimization processes that render normal existing social relations in schools, businesses, hospitals, and other places of work; place the role of ethics and moral imperatives above technical skills and mastery learning; and discover through language new ways to live out personal and social change.

An important emphasis in critical pedagogy (for example, Freire, Giroux, Apple, McLaren) is the transformative power of language to change the status of people in political and social systems. McLaren (1989: 164, 160) writes that critical educators "have responsibility not only for how we act individually in society, but also for the system in which we participate." And further, that "critical researchers have given primacy to the social, the cultural, the political, and the economic, in order to better understand the workings of contemporary schooling." The critique of U.S. schooling by critical pedagogues over the past years has served to heighten our sensitivity to social, political, and educational problems. In addition, from this critique we have learned how difficult it is to change the roles schools play in our society. Although there has been significant headway made in educating many teachers and administrators on the necessity to educate young people to become critical and active citizens, most educators do not see themselves as change advocates. The role most of them fill is one of maintainer or bush fire fighter. Once an educator recognizes problems with the present categories of gender, race, power, and class, the next step is to act. Although new understandings and actions should not be juxtaposed merely in a linear fashion, there is significant merit in Freire's (1973: 44) premise: "to every understanding, sooner or later an action corresponds." The problem for informed and reflective critical educators is the system in which they work. Particularly in large social systems, action that reflects genuine change occurs slowly since educational change usually does not reflect substantial differences in structure or policy from the previous format. An example is the 1991 (and subsequent years) educational response to school problems by "restructuring" the educational system. Even the metaphor, "restructure," tells us it would be more of the same.

In discussing the foundational principles of critical pedagogy, McLaren (1989: 160) introduces them as follows: "Critical pedagogy resonates with the sensibility of the Hebrew symbol 'tikkun,' which means 'to heal, repair, and transform the world. . . .' It provides historical, cultural, political, and ethical direction for those in education who still dare to hope. Irrevocably committed to the side of the oppressed, critical pedagogy is as revolutionary as the earlier views of the authors of the Declaration of Independence: since history is fundamentally open to change, liberation is an authentic goal, and a radically different world can be brought into being." The preceding description sets the tone for critical pedagogy — a region of exploration and life dedicated towards revolutionary action against oppression.

Critical hermeneutics, the undergirding for the present work, relies in a substantial way on the authority of traditions — a region of exploration and life dedicated to reinterpretation of one's cultural heritage and one's self in relationship to others. Critical hermeneutic participatory research is not described as a revolutionary position; rather it is a position to which one is summoned. Ricoeur (1995a: 262) refers to the self who is summoned as the "summoned subject, . . . the self constituted and defined by its position as respondent." We are always in relationship — in our personal life and in our professional life — and are in the position of respondent to the other one. We do not start with the self apart from relatedness, including the self who is the researcher. As researchers, we are always already in relationship with the people with whom we carry out our inquiry. To recognize the summons is to recognize the nature of critical hermeneutic participatory research. This recognition transforms the manner of approaching the issues we investigate and the position of the researcher. The researcher moves from a position of neutral observer or social advocate to a position of being within a transformative act with others. Kathleen Blamey's (1995: 573) description of Ricoeur's approach to research on language serves as a parallel for describing critical hermeneutic participatory research. The research position is "not from above, from some privileged, external perspective, but from within, from a thorough familiarity with the [issues] in question in order to bring out their interconnections, points of accord and conflict." The researcher and the participants mediate through conversations and actions the interconnections, the points of accord and conflict into different narratives that may open more preferred forms of social and communal organizations.

Although it is not the purpose of this book to argue for a conflationist theory or to pose one region superior to the other, it is my goal to offer a way for researchers to help themselves and others to creatively reinterpret their past. When we are able to reinterpret our past and fuse our horizons with other cultures and traditions, then we may be capable of projecting in a concrete and persuasive manner our interest in freedom. It is obvious that simply or solely reinterpreting one's past does not erase the oppressive conditions of many, nor does it establish justice in our societies and organizations. The process of refiguring the future is as critically important.

Ricoeur (1982: 94–100) writes of the appearance of the most formidable difference between the hermeneutical and critical consciousness, in other words, the disagreement between the hermeneutics of tradition and the critique of ideology. He refers to this difference as an "apparent antithesis." Although there is not one meta-system that encompasses both hermeneutics and critical pedagogy or critique of ideology, we can adopt an attitude or gesture toward our research that recognizes that each speaks from a difference place. By so doing, we accept that we always are in a tradition and in a historical process, and that we oppose the state of falsified and manipulated human communication that renders unjust organizations and societies. Both tradition and ideology then can raise legitimate claims. A productive imagination rather than a reproductive imagination in prescribing a new reading of our lives sees that understanding one's past is not an end in itself. An understanding can serve, however, to mediate the past, which can be related to the development of a just social text.

The key factor in critical hermeneutic participatory research is the understanding of language. To think of language as a tool or as structure limits our creativity and binds us to designated acts outside of our being and apart from our history. When we understand that language is an action that is the medium of our lives, we become connected to others in historical and current communities that have a future. Further, our being in the world is revealed historically in and through language as discourse — a concept in the hermeneutic tradition that implies a relationship with an other. Our actions and our reflections on our actions are preceded by a historical community of speakers. Language as action is an event, not a structure or a representational tool. Below is a graphic depiction of an understanding of language in a structuralist tradition and in a hermeneutic tradition. In the structuralist framework, language is thought of as something that structures our world. In the hermeneutic tradition it is thought of as an event.

Structure   Language   **Event**

Structure	Event
timeless	temporal
words have value	words have meaning
a condition for expression	an act of saying
static	creative
systemic	historical

The depiction was drawn from Phelps's (1988: 191–199) discussion on Ricoeur's attempt to reconcile the structuralist and hermeneutic traditions through a dialectic of structure and event. Research in professional fields, for the most part, has as a paradigm the analytical tradition that relies exclusively on the structuralist account of language. The action- and event-oriented fields of education and management are better served with research projects informed by an interpretive tradition with the practical focus of promoting communication, understanding, and community building.

We can establish dialogical communities without traditionally requisite research funds. Although money most certainly makes research easier, it does not ensure viable data. Rather, interest, commitment, and the willingness to learn how to think about the nature of social reality may bring us closer to appropriate research praxis for many of our social problems. Although it would be naive to suggest that we need only language and the ability to envision a difference to change unjust aspects of our society, understanding the role of language, dialogue, and conversation in research is an important beginning. This book seeks to give readers a way of thinking about language and research that can unleash the creative potential of those people in universities, social and educational agencies, and businesses who work with organization and community members to think differently about our social problems and to evaluate wisely and act on new ideas.

[handwritten margin notes: DON'T NEED TO DO MONEY THIS TYPE OF RESEARCH, 2th... IT HELPS / LANGUAGE IS NOT THE ONLY WAY SO... WILL BE CHANGE / IT TAKES MORE / BUT IS NECESSA...]

This book is comprised of three chapters. Chapter 1 recounts some of the problems inherent in the positivist approach to research in social science, followed by an overview of the nature of language in the hermeneutic tradition. Included in this chapter is a discussion on the work, among others, of biologists Humberto Maturana and Francisco Varela on the communicative and social nature of living systems. Their work is discussed to show that not only is the positivist position weak from a philosophical point of view, but this position is also undermined by recent work in the natural sciences. In the early part of the century, logical positivists in several social science fields, such as psychology (Feigl 1970), based their theories on an ideal — the unity of the natural and social sciences. This unity was never achieved because it is impossible within the logical empirical paradigm, for example, to study ball bearings traveling down inclined planes on the one hand, and, on the other hand, moral choices people make in social institutions. This is the case, simply, because ball bearings do not make moral choices. The dominance of the positivist paradigm, for the most part, has shielded us from committing ourselves to other forms of inquiry. Today, if there is any desire to work toward this unity in social science, it would behoove researchers in the positivist tradition, most particularly in applied fields, such as education, nursing, and business, to learn what natural scientists are saying about the nature of language and reality. Further, in Chapter 1, the role of language in communication and policy is discussed.

Chapter 2 examines a history of hermeneutics, language, and understanding as the constitutive core of participatory research. The issuing of questions, assertions, commands, or statements does not change the way we — or others — are in the world. To change ourselves and others is a far more complex activity. However, when we understand the fundamental place of language and conversation in our lives, we see research and our work in organizations, communities, and society in a different light. The discussion of language shows that our traditions and our history have been seriously slighted in favor of technology. In fact, the domination of technology, based on a Newtonian version of science, gives us a false and misleading reliance on the "expert." In our culture, people long for deeper and more relevant meaning in their lives, both public and private, than what the technocratic paradigm has generated in our research and practice. Educators at the university level have a multifaceted responsibility to educate students and others on how to use and reinterpret their history that they may, as Ricoeur writes (1982: 97), be able to "projec[t] concretely [their] interest in emancipation." One of the most important arguments of this book is that today our professional obligations require us to take a different stance than one that simply involves technical or sociological activities found in a survey or in a narrative. We must seek to make explicit what is implicit in our philosophical positions and in our conversations. The critical point is to change relationships among members in organizations and communities. This change does not begin by our changing the other, but by changing oneself.

Chapter 2 also reviews the work of contemporary writers including Heidegger, Gadamer, Habermas, and Ricoeur to frame a philosophical backdrop for participatory research. Although these authors certainly do not all agree, there is a common thread running through their work about the importance of language that brings to consciousness what is needed in our social science research praxis. A critical analysis of these authors' works helps us to understand how we can transcend the dichotomy between what we do in research and who we become in the process.

Chapter 3 provides an overview of the research protocol in field-based critical hermeneutic research. Specific topics include the focus of a research project, research categories, questions and conversations, the selection of participants, entree, background of the researcher, data collection and analysis, and learning and community. Included in this chapter are examples from various research projects on aspects of participatory hermeneutic research.

In embarking on the road of critical and interpretive inquiry, researcher and participants embrace concepts and activities, such as critique and understanding, that are not usually a part of the rationalistic research paradigm. The concepts of reliability, verifiability, simplicity, and repeatability are in stark contrast to critical interpretive inquiry. Numerous discussions and some debate (for example, Eisner and Peshkin [1990]) have emerged from the rationalistic tradition concerning the merits and characteristics of quantitative and qualitative research. However, when the discussions or debates are moved beyond merely the rationalistic framework and are carried to a philosophical level, the issue becomes one of whether research is an epistemological or an ontological enterprise. Moreover, without a reading of hermeneutic literature or philosophy of science, the discussions are grounded in a paradigm that does not allow one to go beyond the level of a dichotomy. In Chapter 3, quantitative and qualitative research in a positivist tradition is compared with participatory research in an interpretive and critical tradition.

Rather than a focus on whether one or the other side of the spurious dichotomy of epistemology (structure, explanation) or ontology (meaning, understanding) should be at the center of our research efforts, the orientation of this book is reflective of Ricoeur's emphasis on the text and the "realization of discourse as text." Within this orientation resides the possibility for a researcher to find structure and explanation embodied in text as a whole work. This orientation is distinct from explaining a text in terms of individual components or in terms of the author's intention. More importantly, this orientation provides the opportunity for anyone to conscientiously and responsibly read a text as an act that recovers its meaning. Neither the author (or researcher) nor the audience for whom the text was written has a privileged role in construing the text's meaning, though at the time the text is created their role in determining meaning is immediate but non-definitive.

Ricoeur's definition of text is discourse fixed in writing. However, in his thinking, a text is more than simply a written sentence, document, or narrative. It is a work defined by its creation, based in a tradition or genre, characterized by a style, and made evident by its use. Explanation and structure of a text are subordinated to an ontology of interpretation and implication — the heart of field-based research in a hermeneutic tradition. In Ricoeur's thinking, text implies several dimensions: composition, work (that is, labor is used in forming language), and inscription. All of these features set the stage for extending the notion of a text to phenomena not limited to writing or even discourse. Text as social action invokes an intimate relation between the theory of interpretation and the social sciences (Ricoeur 1982: 37).

Appropriate responses to our social problems cannot be generated using *techne*. Rather, the subject of ethical reasoning (*phronesis*), although quite new to U.S. social science research, can be found in many conversations and in various program and policy plans. Traditional research designs do not allow for the consideration of the ethical aspects of social problems, those aspects of human life that are most important in the determination of alternative actions. The research process and examples in Chapter 3 position the real problems in organizations and society and provide readers with alternative protocols for future research projects in anticipation of ongoing conversations with colleagues to further our understanding and research practice.

NOTES

1. Participatory research in this book refers to collaborative research carried out in a critical hermeneutic tradition. I use the terms "participatory research," "participatory inquiry," "field-based hermeneutic research," "participatory hermeneutic research," and "applied hermeneutic research" interchangeably. Keiffer distinguishes between participatory and collaborative research. He

suggests that, on the one hand, in collaborative research the researcher and participants both work on problem identification and research design, and, on the other hand, in participatory research the researcher identifies the research problem and design and the participants contribute by discussing the issues, reflecting, and responding to the recorded interviews. I do not use the words participatory and collaborative in these rather specialized senses. I use them to mean collective, joint actions.

Participatory research can be carried out from within different traditions, such as phenomenological, critical pedagogy, or critical hermeneutic. My intention in this book is to bring to the reader the orientation necessary to carry out participatory research from a critical hermeneutic perspective. The term participatory research is becoming a more generic term than it was a few years ago and it can be part of a future discussion delineating differences among participatory research approaches.

2.   When quoting authors who use the male pronoun to embrace both genders, I do not change the original he to read he or she.

1

From a Positivist to an Interpretive Orientation in Research: *Techne, Autopoiesis, Phronesis*

The transition from a focus on logic and technique to an emphasis on understanding and action is beginning to take place, albeit slowly, in the U.S. social science research scene. This chapter looks at some of the implications of the technical and rationalistic approaches to research that are part of the "legacy of logical positivism" (Achinstein & Barker 1969). In addition, discussions on the nature of language as the medium for our social reality set the stage for looking at an example of a social science topic, namely social policy effects on disabled persons.

A TECHNICAL APPROACH

Most researchers in applied social sciences, especially in education, rely on the survey method using statistical techniques for analysis. In the recent past, there has been emphasis on qualitative research approaches, such as grounded theory, ethnography, case histories, and action research. However, whether quantitative or qualitative in approach, language has been assumed to be a representational carrier of meaning, a receptacle that holds words in order to represent the world. This concept of language reflects the basic tenets of logical positivism and derives, for the most part, from logic, the foundations of mathematics, and the paradigm for basic research in the physical sciences. Whether social or non-social phenomena are the focus of inquiry, this Cartesian approach to investigation is based on the presumed discovery of law-like generalizations that serve as the basis for deductive explanation and predictions. Chaney (1974, 1975, 1978, 1983) has argued that the search for universal covering laws is not the question, but rather we should ask why and how variables form universal patterns that influence human behavior and thought. Further, he suggests that the social scientist should shift attention from law-between-the-variables within a space-time framework to a meta-framework that addresses the multitude of ways in which people give meaning to their actions and the consequences of these actions.

From within a tradition of critical theory, many social scientists and philosophers over the last several generations have critiqued the positivist framework as a basis for research in social science. For the most part, until recently, critique of the Cartesian philosophy, especially in applied fields, such as education, business, and nursing, has taken place in other countries than the United States. This is now changing. For example, we see inroads having been made for several years by researchers, such as Michael Apple, David Allen, C. A. Bowers, Robert Everhart, William Foster, Henry Giroux, and Janet Thompson, who apply a critical approach to their investigations. One of the earliest social scientists in adult education to write from a critical perspective is Paulo Freire.

The idea of critique or critical continues to catch on. Although there recently has been a surge of workshops, books, and consultants teaching critical thinking skills to U.S. educators in various fields, these skills, as they are understood and taught, have little to do with critique. As P. McLaren (1989: 161) points out in *Life in Schools*, the term "critical" has been neutralized by repeated and imprecise usage, thus removing the political and cultural dimensions from thinking skills. Elaborating on this observation, it can be said that critical thinking skills only refer to one type of thinking skills, namely analytical. Unless there is a reflective and historical dimension to our thinking, it will not change how we reason and how we live out our lives. The critical thinking mentality that is sweeping our educational organizations has bewildered and distorted what kind of thinking we actually need in order for our understanding of social, economical, moral problems to change. The lack of depth of the current usage of the term "thinking" in the critical thinking bandwagon undermines the potential of adult or young learners to reflect, learn, and act in meaningful ways.

Although writing about critique is now prevalent in U.S. journals of social science, it is difficult to move beyond critique into practice. The preparation programs for graduate students in social sciences, teachers in education, and leaders in organizations and communities need to portray the value and necessity of critique that in turn would lead to vastly different agendas in social research. The difficulty lies in disinterest in, or perhaps fear of, learning about and living in new paradigms of philosophical, academic, and practical inquiry. To move beyond the one dominant positivist paradigm for social science research, particularly in applied social sciences, we need to see value in learning new ideas and in embracing different choices that allow learners to be exposed to new ways to think about data, research, language, and meaning.

Although few researchers will admit to being positivists, the "legacy of logical positivism" still pervades contemporary social inquiry today. For positivists, the relation of theory to practice is chiefly technical, because they seek to use general laws and manipulate a desired state of affairs. However, the question of which state of affairs should be produced is not to be resolved scientifically. No ought can be derived from an is, and no value can be derived from a fact. Scientific inquiry is value-free within this framework, whereby the empirical basis of science is composed of observable objects or events that, in turn, serve as part of the program for a unity of science.

Many writers have critiqued this rationality and have demonstrated problems with using the logical positivist frameworks as the basis for social inquiry. These writers include those who use phenomenological and ethnomethodological approaches that developed out of the works of Husserl and Schutz, those who have taken a linguistic approach based on the influence of Wittgenstein's later work, those who have drawn their rationale from a Marxist tradition, and those who have advocated the hermeneutic approach influenced by Heidegger. The common element in all these traditions is the recognition that the positivist approach has neglected the meanings that are at the basis of social reality. They have argued that access to a symbolically structured domain calls for procedures more closely aligned with those developed in philosophy and the humanities than those developed in traditional physical-biological sciences. As Bernstein (1983: xi) notes, this tradition opens the way "to a more historically situated, nonalgorithmic, flexible understanding of human rationality, one which highlights the tacit dimension of human judgment and imagination and is sensitive to the unsuspected contingencies and genuine novelties encountered in particular situations."

The fundamental problem with the logical positivist way of thinking is the attempt to reduce meaning to behavior. When social scientists try to do this, they deny the internal relationship between ideas and action. This is a crucial oversight because thought is a basic component in generating behavior. Action and ideas are not independent of each other.

Actions express intentions that cannot be comprehended independently of language.

The attempt of positivists to understand human problems using technical procedures has obscured this issue. Traditionally, these social scientists have thought that they could solve practical problems simply by applying their knowledge to the problem, thereby reducing practical issues to a question of applying the right technique. Habermas (1973: 255) makes this point forcefully when he writes (1973a: 255) about modern society's failure to distinguish between the practical and technical; thus,

The real difficulty in the relation of theory to praxis does not arise from this new function of science as technologic force, but rather from the fact that we are no longer able to distinguish between practical and technical power. Yet even a civilization that has been rendered scientific is not granted dispensation from practical questions: therefore a peculiar danger arises when the process of scientification transgresses the limit of reflection of a rationality confined to the technological horizon. For then no attempt at all is made to attain a rational consensus on the part of citizens concerned with the practical control of their destiny. Its place is taken by the attempt to attain technical control over history by perfecting the administration of society, an attempt that is just as impractical as it is unhistorical.

The prevailing tendency to reduce problems of actions to problems of technical control and manipulation results in power being taken away from the people who have the problems and who need to develop capacities for solving them. This results in what Habermas (1970: 75) refers to as the "depoliticization of the mass of the population and the decline of the political realm as a political institution." As he points out, when there is an absence of practical discourse among the public realm, it loses its function. This problem is urgent, particularly in advanced industrial countries where technological consciousness increasingly dominates most realms of human society. However, we see problems similar to this in developing nations as they strive to modernize and imitate industrialized nations in that they confuse needs with wants. In Chapter 3 some examples speak directly to this issue. As international business relationships develop and mature, they bring in more capital and buying power for everyday people along with unchallenged Western values of materialism and individualism. We need to learn how to identify genuine needs at particular times. For example, simply building a modern hospital and supplying advanced technology do not necessarily support social and economic development in ways that might better address local needs.

In Western industrialized countries as well as in many developing countries, community and society cohesiveness and purpose suffer at the expense of advancing technology because technological advances rely on skill and technique. Instead, living out a meaningful life in our organizations, communities, and society relies on moral and political imperatives. When we attempt to develop our organizations, communities, cities, and nations through technological advances only, the social and communal integration breakdowns drastically offset technological expansion. Although we may agree this is the high price many nations are paying for westernization, which is what modernization often entails, we nonetheless still adhere to the same assumptions and tacit mindset found in our ideas about innovation and technological advance. Mander (1991: 22, 23) portrays the traps in our reasoning: "technological innovation is good. It is always good. It aids health. It saves labor. It is the engine that drives economic growth . . . which is a benefit to all people. Technical innovation promotes democracy, freedom and leisure. Technical progress will spread around the world and relieve all people of the awful toil that has oppressed man since the dawn of time."

We have long equated technological innovation with human progress. Further, scientific metaphors have structured our thinking — input, interface, functional, system, network, output — and most do not engender critical reflection or an ethical stance. Our language reflects our values and priorities. We question our values and priorities when we see that control, violence, illness, disposal, and sex serve as the coins for computer terms — crash, boot, abort, access, security, password, virus, infected, virulent, contagious, sterilize, hard disk, floppy disk, dump, and trash.

We presume the computer has the attributes of mind, such as memory, and the human mind has the attributes of a computer, including information storage and data processing. There is the position held by Nadeau (1991: 171) that "human beings are programmed in a manner analogous to programming computers. The hardware that is our brain allows us to assimilate the software of language and this software becomes the basis for encoding all aspects of the elaborate software package of a transmitted culture."

This position dangerously ignores the nature and importance of reason spanning both technical and moral imperatives as noted by Bellah and colleagues (1991: 44) who point out the profound gap "between technical reason, the knowledge with which we design computers or analyze the structure of DNA, and practical or moral reason, the ways we understand how we should live. . . .What we need to know is not simply how to build a powerful computer or how to redesign DNA but precisely and above all what to do with that knowledge."

The challenge is both what to do with our knowledge and how to refigure the current disparities and contradictions of our lives housed in our language and actions. To meet the challenge calls for a rethinking of the core of our humanness, a questioning of the nature of our identity (see Herda 1997). The fundamental question of identity is resolved not by an answer so much as by an orientation, a stance toward the other in our organizations and communities. We cannot separate our basic ontological nature from our research as social scientists. To authentically address our local and global challenges, we must move beyond changing our techniques in research to changing first ourselves as researchers.

An alternative to the positivist approach in research does not begin simply when qualitative research methodologies are used, such as open-ended interviews or when ethnographies are carried out. Ethnography may be carried out within one of several paradigms, including a positivist, a phenomenological, or an interpretative paradigm. It is not a matter of applying new tools to an old trade in the move from one paradigm to another. Researchers move from one paradigm to another when their thinking and reasoning change. In the move from a positivist to an interpretive paradigm, researchers understand the relationship between themselves and others not merely from a subject-object distinction, or an intersubjective phenomenology, but from an acknowledgment that the other is a critical part of their own identity.[1]

The difference between a positivist approach and an interpretative approach, most simply stated, is in how language is viewed — language as a tool representing the world or language as a medium through which we interpret and begin to change our selves and our conditions. This medium brings us to the place of conversation and the domain of the text that gives us the capacity to redescribe or refigure our everyday world in organizations and communities. It is in this redescription where social action, which moves beyond old behaviors and worn-out traditions, has its genesis. An interpersonal relationship among the researcher and participants is inherent in the research act and by virtue of the nature of this act — a moral rather than a technical act — orients the analysis of data toward the practical world of both the researcher and the participants.

A LANGUAGE APPROACH

The conditions of human society in which forms of social texts are situated cannot be transposed unaltered into actions that obey specific rules.

The facts derived from a study of behavior shield from us those facets of everyday life and practice that are most important in understanding the meanings of our actions. A study of social texts must be an interpretive activity that takes into account beliefs, traditions, our imagination, and the consequences of our acts.

Increasingly, in philosophy and social sciences we see the role of language taking on relevance for those working with institutional concerns, such as organizational development, policy analysis, and education. We also see research in the natural sciences, such as biology, supporting the idea that humans think, act, and change their lives in language and communication (for example, Winograd and Flores [1986] discuss these topics directed to management theory and computers).

Humberto R. Maturana, the Chilean biologist, writes at length on the creation of language systems by human organisms. In his view, language is formed and shaped within social structure rather than in the cognitive structures of individuals. This occurs, he asserts, because language is created through a process of "mutual orientation." It is not grounded in a direct representation of the world; rather, it is created and expressed as a "consensual domain" between individuals who are part of a social network and participate together in interlinked patterns of activity. Consequently, language is never something that is purely descriptive or that simply *is*. Language becomes a form of action, as described by Habermas (1979) who emphasizes the act of language instead of its representational role. Just as social life is always in a process of change and becoming, so is language. It connects the actors in society and is continually being formed through anticipation and the process of consensuality about what language is and what it creates. As Maturana (1980: 41) points out, humans exist in a linguistic, cognitive domain.

Maturana and Varela (1980: 45–46) describe the continual process of the transformation of the domains as a learning process. Learning as understood by Maturana is not an accumulation of representations of the environment. It is the continual process of behavior through change in the system's capacity to self-organize and reorient. The system, at any given time, contains both the limits and the potential for transformation. The description of such systems cannot be accomplished by independent, outside observation. In a dependent, self-referring system, such as a living system, the situation is different. Here, observers can only describe their interactions in the parts that they define. Definition, and hence meaning, is disclosed through interactions. These interactions are a unity that can only be transformed or changed when relationships between parts change. The implication for research is that researchers and participants are connected observers in a single unity. They together necessarily disclose through definition a unity that changes only when the relationships between researcher and participants change.

Maturana characterizes the identity of living systems as being constituted by interactions and transformations and, in the process, our understandings. This implies that we are always on the way to renewal and the creation of a self-knowledge that is achieved by dialectical interplay with the "other." In carrying this characterization into an investigation of sociocultural phenomena, we see that the process of identity, described by Maturana, is not unlike Gadamer's account of history and the nature of situated relationships throughout time. Gadamer speaks of a historical object not as an object at all but as the unity of the one and the other. Both the history and the understanding of the history exist in this same kind of unity. He suggests that a proper hermeneutics, a proper way to understand relationships, might demonstrate the effectivity of history within understanding itself. For two situations, or unities, to know each other, or understand each other, requires a particular achievement, mainly the "fusion of horizons." Therefore, to describe a unity or situation, it is necessary to see it from a particular standpoint within a set of particular standpoints.

Language not only helps to define the social world for the participants in it but also is essential for creating that world. Language does more than enable us to comprehend or represent this world and our understanding of it. Language plays a generative role in enabling us to create and acknowledge meaning as we engage in discourse and fulfill social obligations, which have, in turn, been created through language. Thus, these social obligations are characterized as moral activities; the simple fulfillment of an obligation does not release us from the implications for others that our actions might have.

Most typically, we take for granted our social actions, structured or patterned by language, and we fail to see them. However, when there are breakdowns in communication, we have the opportunity to become disengaged from unquestioned and taken-for-granted activities. This disengagement may enable us to see more clearly the structural domain that gives meaning to language. This is not unlike Heidegger's idea of "throwness" of a person. Upon reflection and acknowledgment of disturbances or breakdowns in the understanding and activities of our everyday life, we can stand in a new relationship to ourselves and others. The aspects of throwness and language in Heidegger's work are further discussed below and in Chapter 2.

Another key point, deriving from the recognition that language is situated in a social structure rather than in the cognition of an individual, is that we can control the direction of our own creation —an idea that has major implications for the development of organizations and social policy. In other words, our words are what contribute to creating the world we live in, rather than developing to fit the world (Searle 1979). This means that we play a dynamic and crucial role in shaping our own structures and processes whether we are aware of doing this or not. However, through such awareness, we can consciously exercise more control over this directional process, rather than letting it emerge as the result of a series of uncoordinated human language events.

In the past, social science thinking has been guided by the rationalistic tradition that takes language as a representational carrier of meaning and conceals its central social role. Now we need to recognize the dynamic, creational capabilities of language. We need to be engaged, committed, and thereby consciously able to assume the role of creator and evaluator of our social conventions and obligations. When we do make use of our ability to create and accept, or decline, obligations, we are more fully using language as it has the potential to be used. When we understand language in this ontological sense, our work in applied hermeneutic research can help to shape a context in which we can change. In this same context, others can change, and new understandings and new insights into our social problems can emerge.

Maturana suggests we can escape our past constrictions in using language fully in two ways: by moving beyond the role of the observer to create phenomenal domains in which our participation is essential and by taking advantage of the process of structural coupling, whereby social links give rise to changes in the direction of social activity. In other words, through the more active use of language, we can take a more active role in shaping our history and interpersonal lives.

Another key principle that flows out of this understanding of the creative use of language is the recognition, suggested by Heidegger, that the interpreter (or actor) and the interpreted (the world) are not independent of each other but are interlinked. This means that existence and interpretation are interdependent, for we are continually in the act of interpreting our own existence. This also means that prejudice or bias becomes a necessary part of the act of interpretation, because we bring our background and being to the act. As Gadamer (1976: 9) says, our prejudices or biases represent our openness to the world. They are the conditions under which we experience something and whereby what we encounter says something to us. Similarly, Heidegger (1962: 188–197) asserts that when something is to be understood, it is to be unveiled, or interpreted, which happens by an act of appropriation that, in turn, "is always done under the guidance of a point of view."

The position we take in interpreting our world comes from the social domain in which we operate, because meaning is fundamentally social and cannot be determined by referring to the meaning-giving activity of individual subjects. Individuals are linked to others in a social system that is constantly in the process of being created through language acts. The positivist research stance of neutrality shields researchers from critical elements in the research act — recognition of their constitutive role in the research process and acknowledgment of their moral obligation in experiencing anything.

Traditionally, we have examined language by studying the characteristics of an individual language learner or language user, but as Heidegger argues, this is an inappropriate starting point. Instead, we must use social actions, not individual actions, as a starting point in understanding intelligibility and even existence (Heidegger 1971).

The language we learn has its roots in the social environment in which we learn it. Yet, we are never locked within a single grammar, or a particular understanding, because the first language we learn also puts us in a position to step out of that language to interpret and critique our present and our past. Although we are shaped by our historical roots, and derive our prejudices and biases in interpretation from those roots, we can also go beyond them to create new structure and language systems when we interact with others. Language is a form of action. Whether what you say is taken for granted or whether it is used to form the basis for an argument, the act of making the utterance creates the objects and properties it describes for both the speaker and the hearer. When we make statements that refer to altering and changing our social context, those statements, themselves, contribute significantly to a basis for personal and social change.

These statements involve consensus with others, because as previously noted, Maturana emphasizes that we create our concepts and make the observations we do within a consensual domain. Alternatively, as Heidegger (1971: 40) observes, "man stands in a relationship." Whenever we make a descriptive statement, whether we are talking about the domain of goals and intentions or physical systems, we are inevitably making a statement through which one observer communicates with another observer. For mutual understanding, there must be consensuality, for this statement is not grounded in the external reality, which we only think about and define through our statements, but in the consensual domain shared by those observers about that reality. In other words, the properties of things

— and, in fact, the recognition of distinct things at all — exist only as operational distinctions that we make as observers in talking about reality. We create our own domain of distinctions through language, and, most crucially, as Maturana emphasizes, we must recognize that these distinctions derive from the consensual domain. They come about because of some kind of interaction in which the observer is engaged. Maturana (1978: 44) writes that: "The linguistic domain as a domain of orienting behavior requires at least two interacting organisms with comparable domains of interaction, so that a cooperative system of consensual interactions may be developed in which the emerging conduct of the two organisms is relevant for both. The central feature of human existence is its occurrence in a linguistic cognitive domain. This domain is constitutively social." Reality is neither objective nor does it derive from the individual alone. It results from a consensuality or mutuality of observation that itself results from social interaction among individuals inextricably linked in a network of social connections.

In the process of using and sharing this language with others, each individual is actively engaged within that language, as part of a language community, or as Heidegger (1962: 175–180 margination (218–224 pagination)) asserts, the feature of all language activity (the process of both saying and listening) is the engagement of the person within language — a concept he refers to as the "throwness of the person with language." Throwness means the coming to be in a situation of specified and ongoing histories. Because we come to be within ongoing traditions and prejudices, we cannot succeed in the Cartesian philosophy of neutrally choosing a place from which to begin our plans or our research. With such a line of reasoning, one can see the intimate relationship between language and research in looking back with historical perspective and looking forward to what might be possible implications for the research data.

Building on Heidegger's work on the relationship between humans and language, Gadamer (1988) carries the reasoning further about the centrality of language and posits that language has its true being only in conversation that is the exercise of understanding between people. Language is not merely a set of tools needed for communication. In a similar way, neither is communication limited to mean an exchange of information or an exercise of understanding people merely expressing their will to each other. Rather, communication for Gadamer (1988: 404) is a much deeper topic, an ontological event; "It is a living process in which a community of life is lived out." In linguistic communication, a world is disclosed that "sets its theme before those communicating like a disputed object between them. . . . Thus the world is a common ground, trodden by none and recognized by all, uniting all who speak with one another. All forms of human community of life are forms of linguistic community: even more, they constitute language, but it acquires its reality only in the process of communicating. That is why it is not a mere means of communication."

People of different traditions and different histories come to us with a linguistically constituted world that presents itself to us. This world is always open to new insights, "and hence for every expansion of its own world picture, and accordingly available to others" (Gadamer 1988: 405). Within this philosophical framework, transnational and transcultural understanding is possible in community, not merely in an exchange of information or in cultural sensitivity-training sessions.

Both Gadamer and Habermas use linguistics as the point of departure for their programs. Although Gadamer works in an ontological framework, Habermas develops an epistemological process. While Gadamer works on the continuum between ontology and methods of discovering truth, Habermas's research leads toward an epistemology of methods. They both agree that it is not feasible to split the subject and object as in Kantian tradition, that truth is bedded in a language and conversation, and that the moral issues in social life can be made explicit only in application. Habermas's theory begins with the act of communication in which rationality and morality are embedded.

According to Habermas's theory (1979), in the course of communicating with others, the person raises universal validity claims, based on whether others can agree with the language the person uses, as well as with the content communicated by that language. For Habermas (1979, 1984), the agreement that people reach in using language is based on the recognition by others of the validity of their claims, and their potential redemption, in language use to comprehensibility, shared knowledge, trust or sincerity, and shared norms or values.

Another way of looking at this analysis is to say the world is always organized around fundamental concerns that derive from or are expressed through language, such as human understanding, prejudices, and interests. The world depends for its continued existence upon these projects that give it being and organization. Within this dynamic system, which is always in the process of being created, meaning is continually created through a mutual interchange involving active listening and speaking, which in turn provoke interpretation. Meaning derives through our engagement and commitment to the world and our interaction with others.

When we encounter the world, we do so as something that has already been lived in and acted upon. In our own encounter, we act upon it, and the process by which we act on it develops out of our own understanding.

This orients us to the world both as it exists and as it has the potential to become. It is as if, as Ricoeur (1982: 57) reminds us, we have before us the opportunity to understand, shape, and direct "the structure of being which underlies the problem of choice." We have this possibility because we can use the process of interpretation to project a possible world, a potential mode of human existence. From the standpoint of Ricoeur (1982: 56), understanding "is not concerned with grasping a fact but with apprehending a possibility of being."

LANGUAGE AND POLICY

The ontological nature of understanding and the shared and dynamic role of language in society should, in turn, lead us to examine our values, beliefs, and traditions, because we all are subject to our conscious decision to change them for different policies or for different relationships with other members of an organization or community. Nevertheless, our values, beliefs, and traditions often are not examined critically. A study of language and symbols can lead to an investigation of beliefs, for example, that are taken for granted. In policy matters, the belief in the utility of a government program or law, the assignment of responsibility for the success or failure of social-implementation programs, or the belief in the salience of a course of action often are uncritically accepted by members of the political groups that create the program.

Vivid metaphors, very often in statistical form, create benchmarks that shape popular opinions and cause people to judge certain policies or programs as successful or not. The metaphor welfare suggests an aid in the well-being of certain people. However, welfare programs carry with them more implications than just helping people. There is the overwhelming bureaucracy associated with welfare that prevents some from receiving aid and allows others to receive more than their due. When government officials develop a plan to reduce unemployment or hold an expected increase below a cheering percentage, this plan itself creates an ideal of success to be used in evaluating future trends. The policy-makers focus their attention and the attention of their constituents on the publicized goal rather than on the problem itself (that is, several million people without jobs). This attitude, in turn, leads to incremental policy changes, but it masks whatever underlies the increments and consequently what the politicians and policy member should consider. As Edelman (1977: 37) points out, officials and the public become concerned with the symbol rather than the substance. He writes:

To publicize incremental changes in policy or in well-being is to establish categories that conceal the institutional context in which the problem is grounded. This form of structuring of a problem always produces symbolic or token gestures; for officials and the public who are attentive to the increments perceive these as the core of the issue while remaining largely oblivious to whatever problems underlie the increments. Each symbolic gesture further reinforces the categorization scheme and the associated definition of the situation.

Policy-makers and the public become attached to metaphors that actually shield the discordant meanings of particular policies and programs. Unfortunately, the irony of this is that metaphors can be most effective when they are "wrong" (Percy 1958: 79–99). As Geertz (1973: 210) points out, metaphor has "a stratification of meaning, in which an incongruity of sense on one level produces an influx of significance on another." People can attempt to make sense out of something that does not otherwise make sense and thus imbue it with new meanings. Or people can become disturbed by the incongruities of public policies and political facts, and their dissatisfaction can lead to conflict that could, in turn, result in evaluation and negotiation over alternative courses of action. Their acceptance of a certain metaphoric representation can lead them to forget there is a problem or make them believe that significant change or progress is occurring to either curb the problem or prevent it from getting worse. Geertz (1973: 211) describes this transformation process succinctly when he writes that when "it works, a metaphor transforms a false identification (for example, of the labor policies of the Republican Party and those of the Bolsheviks) into an apt analogy; when it misfires, it is mere extravagance."

Symbols and metaphors likewise influence our interpretation of political issues and our actions because we derive our ideas about what our problems are and the nature of the solutions from subtle linguistic evocations and associated government actions. We respond to cues that lead us to judge public policies. We respond in this way because language and symbols define the boundaries of our political realities (see Edelman 1988: 103–119). For example, we have certain simple images for comprehending complex entities like the "helping professions," "welfare," "least restrictive environment (for the handicapped)," or "defense budget" because it is easier to understand when we use linguistic codes. However, in reality, the complexity of such institutional constructs demands an analysis that penetrates beyond the current, dominant research modes, namely survey research and statistical analysis. An analysis should take into account the structures of the meanings underlying the events and concepts that are part of the problems. Geertz (1973: 213) stresses this need for a more in-depth analysis when he explains, "Not only is the semantic structure of the figure a good deal more complex than it appears on the surface, but an analysis of that structure forces one into tracing a multiplicity of referential connections between it and social reality, so that the final picture is one of configuration of dissimilar meanings out of whose interworking both the expressive power and the rhetorical force of the final symbol derive."

Through in-depth analysis, a social researcher can uncover significant meanings behind the metaphors, symbols, and codes and make these underlying meanings more obvious for conscious consideration. In doing this, the researcher participates in a social process, because the revelation of meanings does not occur as a result of abstract reasoning or formulations. Geertz (1973: 213) in his discussion on the interactive nature of symbolic analysis notes, drawing from Percy, that symbolic analysis relies on a social process that is "not 'in the head,' but in that public world where 'people talk together, name things, make assertions, and to a degree understand each other'." Social science research into current policy issues cannot be a technical science trying to uncover statistical generalizations or intervention mechanisms but primarily must be an interpretive science through which the researcher searches for meanings and engages in critical discourse characterized by ethical considerations with those who are part of the research project. The move from research based in *techne* to one based in *phronesis* is a conscious move and a moral decision. In policy research it is most often a move from functionalist-based research to interpretive research. In policy analysis, the historical background of a problem is frequently not considered. Traditional functionalism couched in an evolutionary model is the basis for most policy design. Below is an example in which history and interpretation are used in an analysis of a social policy issue to aid handicapped individuals.

DISABILITY AND BEING IN SAMOA

When we study how Samoans live with disabled members of their culture, and compare these practices with those in our culture, we can learn from them. We not only become aware of the vast differences or variability of behavior, but we also discover how the Samoans think differently than we do about disability. Our prejudgments influence our social policy practices and are reflected in our language.

Until recently there were no special places in Samoa to send disabled people. However, few families relinquish caring for their disabled family member. In highly industrialized countries, for example Germany, disabled persons often either are physically or psychologically separated from families and communities. Other countries, such as the United States, have made major efforts to pass and implement laws based on inclusiveness. A major difference between industrialized countries and industrializing countries is that the family unit (for example, in Samoa) is the basis of each individual's being or identity in contrast with the emphasis on individualism in many Western countries. In Samoa, once you are a member of the family, you are always a member of the family whether you are disabled or die; the disabled person receives no special status, in the same way that the dead person is considered an ongoing part of the family. For instance, a family will bury the dead in its front yard, but will still consider the person present. In fact, some living members of the family may lie down on the grave to talk to the deceased family member. Other family members will continue to talk about them as if they were still living, because the deceased individuals are members of the family first and only secondarily characterized as being among the nonliving. In turn, their conception of time reflects this sense of continually being a part of the family too, because there is no past or future in their language, only a present. In talking about a nonliving brother, the Samoans would describe him as if he still possesses the same attributes he did while alive. For instance, a Samoan might say, "My brother, who is dead, has many lands and a lake. He is always joyful." That he is dead is less important than that he is a member of the family. This same perspective characterizes the way Samoans relate to the disabled person. Each person is a family member first.

The place of the disabled family member in Samoa is quite different than in the West, where individuality is touted so highly. This individuality-based rationality has created problems for the Western developers who are trying to establish Independent Living Centers in Samoa, using the same approach that has been used in the West. Because the Samoan family does not separate their disabled from themselves, they are not interested in having their disabled family member go into the center. They are interested, however, in the fact that their family member, who happens to be disabled, will be given a government job, which will bring more money and security to the family. They are happy about this chance to work for the government, which they see as a family endeavor rather than a place to care for the disabled.

This difference in point of view between Samoa and the West can, in turn, teach us some important lessons in living with the disabled and currently able-bodied members of our own society. It shows us that our attempts to legislate equality for the disabled and able-bodied might be misdirected. In fact, we may be trying to force the disabled into a mold into which they may not want to go or cannot go.

This demonstrates the problems that social policy analysts have in using an objective-subjective perspective in assessing what is appropriate for a particular group rather than looking at that group in terms of the possibility of being or in terms of that group's own system of meaning. Although the disabled in our culture do not fit the traditional description of a culture, they have become separate from the rest of our culture in many ways because we have given them a label, disabled, that distinguishes them.

We need to consider shifting our own perspective to view them from the standpoint of being. By doing so, we can change the way we polarize disability and ability into two separate categories, based on a condition of either being perfect or normal (not disabled) or not perfect and not normal (disabled), to a condition of temporariness of being. From this perspective, we are all potentially disabled, and therefore our arrangements to live with the disabled should be designed from this point of view. This is quite different from our present attitude, where we take the position we should try to accept the disabled, because it is the moral, right thing to do, when financially we can afford it. By contrast, if we work out a system of being based on responding to what the temporarily disabled need and want, we are recognizing that the disabled are a part of all of us, not a separate category of being, and all of us can pass in and out of this category at any time. This way we respond based on the disabled being part of the human family to which we all belong, rather than out of feelings of moral obligation or guilt.

Because our responses in the real world are affected by our theoretical perspective, our ideas about knowledge and feelings are thus critical for the way we respond. Although a distinction between discerning fact or ways of being might seem academic — and it does become so when critical theorists and hermeneutic researchers analyze these concepts — this distinction does have pragmatic implications for our understanding of the role of hermeneutic inquiry and its influence on daily life. Our beliefs affect what we do. For example, if we believe that we can change ourselves and help set up the conditions whereby others can change with us, we act differently than if we are interested solely in producing facts or knowledge without considering the applications or implication of our actions. When we do not address implications, we have made a choice, too. Then we only think abstractly about society and use our knowledge for solely academic ends.

Our choices to influence society, should we choose to make them, are influenced by the context of the society in which we make them. For example, we cannot think about disabled in the family context as the Samoans do because we are not Samoans. We can, however, do something with the understandings we have gained about Samoans' beliefs concerning what it is to be human in order to influence the situation affecting the disabled in our own country for the benefit of all. We need to do more than simply collect information to add to our knowledge base; we should also examine the implications of this knowledge for our own lives and act accordingly. Our research models influence the shape of our society.

Maturana and Varela (1980) show this fit between our models and our present society when they suggest that humankind has been continually searching for values and models that explain or justify the human situation. They use the example of the evolutionary model as a case in point, on the grounds that it provided the scientists and others who accepted it with a biological framework that justified the economic and social structure, and that it was likewise based on "survival of the fittest" patterns of behavior. Specifically, Maturana and Varela (1980: 117) write that,

In fact, the social history of man shows a continuous search for values that explain or justify human existence, as well as a continuous use of subordination and political submission of the individuals, isolated or collectively, to the design or whim of those who pretend to represent the values contained in those notions. For a society based on economic discrimination, competitive ideas of power and subordination of the citizen to the state, the notions of evolution, natural selection and fitness (with their emphasis on the species as the perduring historical entity maintained through the dispensability of transient individuals) seemed to provide a biological (scientific) justification for its economic and social structure.

The relationship between the policy we have used in responding to the disabled and the premises underlying that policy have been informed by the variation and selective retention model. We have categorized the disabled from a structural point of view, in the same way that we have created categories of groups along the evolutionary scale.

There are two important implications for social scientists that follow from these ideas about the effects of our models. One implication is that when we rely on form or morphology to understand the selection process, we limit our understanding of what evolves to form and do not take into consideration the diverse qualities that are a part of life. For example, in using the morphology concept, we ignore the diversity of sentiment, emotions, interests, and prejudices of individuals. Instead, we mold everything together into a morphological composite, and we develop our ideas about policies and values based on this creation. The result is a restrictive approach to developing social policy. Instead, we need to think about a more dynamic, process-oriented approach, so we can consider and discuss the various perspectives and positions that are possible for educating ourselves and others and thereby reorganize the ways we presently conceive of and categorize the activities we consider education.

The second implication of using this structural model of understanding is that this model prevents us from understanding the interactive nature of meaning. Instead, we focus on structure, not the dynamic interchange that goes on among individuals involved in the interaction process. Consequently, we miss a great deal, because human interaction is what sets the stage for many forms of sentiments, emotions, and interests to be expressed. If we follow an adaptation model, by contrast, we claim that the organism's structure will respond to the environment by selecting the best form of adaptation to it and will therefore achieve a degree of stabilization within a given environmental setting. Believing that this stabilization occurs, we look for a structural form to explain our progress.

This approach limits us to look for formal structures. If we realized that organisms and their reactions to the environment were constantly unstable and in flux, and if we realized that the environment was similarly undergoing change, then we would understand that we should not look for such structures and expect these forms to occur due to adaptation. Instead, we would realize that all life is informed by an ongoing process of interaction and cooperative change, and this shift in perspective would allow us to take into consideration the diverse emotions, ambitions, and interests of individuals in looking at how the evolutionary process occurs.

Biologically, it may be true that competition contributes to the evolutionary-change process. According to the laws of natural selection, individual members of a species who have the features that are favorably selected are more apt to survive, as are the individuals who gain reproductive advantages over others. Conversely, those who do not survive tend to have less favorable forms of these traits.

From the Darwinian perspective, these facts suggest that the role of the individual is to contribute to perpetuating the species, and that if the natural phenomena follow their ordinary course of development, that will automatically contribute to the further progress of humankind. The biological sciences appeared to justify the belief that any evolutionary change would be for the benefit of mankind.

Maturana and Varela have shown, however, that these arguments are not valid to justify the subordination of the individual to the species. This is the case because the biological phenomenon is determined by the phenomenology of individuals, and without individuals, there is not biological phenomenology. This occurs because the ongoing organization of the individual is autopoietic or self-organizing, meaning that the individual can play a role in creating organization so that humankind becomes defined through its existing, not its existence. Maturana and Varela (1980: 118) claim we cannot consider individuals dispensable for the benefit of the species; all individuals contribute in some measure to this ongoing process. They write: "Thus, biology cannot be used anymore to justify the dispensability of the individuals for the benefit of the species, society, or mankind under the pretense that its role is to perpetuate them. Biologically, the individuals are not dispensable."

The disabled assume a different role, both socially and politically, within the context of Maturana's and Varela's biology than in the Darwinian evolutionary model. Maturana and Varela assert that every type of being is important and plays a part in the grand scheme of things. The disabled also play their part. From this perspective, we should bring the disabled into our mainstream — not because it is our moral obligation to do so, but rather, because they are part of the overall project of humankind, and without them, part of our existing is incomplete.

This understanding leads us to reexamine our ideas about science and reminds us that at the heart of science is our ability to code, classify, and send messages in one form or another. The way we have responded to the disabled provides a good example of this, in that we have classified them for placement in educational settings, for receiving funds to take care of their problem, and for diagnosing their difficulty, so we may assist them. However, our new conception of the diversity of humankind should lead us to recognize our concept of coding as a cognitive notion, one "which represents the interactions of the observer, not a phenomenon operative in the physical domain," as Maturana and Varela (1980: 68) point out. As they explain, "Notions such as coding, message, or information are not applicable to the phenomenon of self-production" (1980: 102). What they mean by this is that we cannot properly use rigid coding to categorize the process of self-organization, because it is a dynamic process. Living systems are created through social or linguistic means. Reproduction, which we have considered at the core of living systems, is not a necessary defining feature of the organization of that system. As the authors explain, "A linguistic domain . . . is intrinsically non-informative" (1980: 120).

These ideas about information are virtually antithetical to the concepts presented in most advanced information and cybernetic theories. Information, which includes codes, messages, and mappings, has been considered the essence of science. It has been the building block from which scientific systems have progressed and evolved through the acquisition of new knowledge. For example, the process of reproduction involves passing on a DNA code from an aging set of tissues to an embryonic set of tissues, and what has mattered for the survival of the species has been the transmittal and survival of the code, because the tissues die each generation, although the code passes on, or so we believe. From the perspective of Darwinian biology, the individual is viewed as insignificant because the code is the basis of the species.

Now a new generation of scientists is questioning the subordination of the individual to the species and protesting a science that submerges the individual in this way. For instance, Sir Stafford Beers (1980: 69) points out that we have invented codes to describe the operations of nature as we perceive it, and we have set up a situation in which our own identity vanishes. However, it does not have to be. As he observes in the preface to *Autopoiesis*, our concern with the code "is why identity vanishes in an ageless computer program and bits — a program that specifies the hydrogen-bonded base pairs that link with sugar-phosphate backbones of the DNA molecule." Then he rejects this over-concern with codes when he points out that, "Nature is not about codes: we observers invent the codes in order to codify what nature is about."

We invent codes to categorize ourselves, although human nature is so diverse that it is even less susceptible to coding. The autopoietic view of biology brings us face-to-face with the issue of identity and lets us realize that the subordination of the individual to the group can no longer be supported. We create a group and assign the individual to it. However, the individual has integrity that exists apart from the group or category we have created for our own convenience and sense of order. A label, for example of a learning disability, follows a child throughout school and often prevents a full opportunity for successful transformation into adulthood.

From an autopoietic perspective, the disabled person should be seen as an individual who has identity in being, not from belonging to a group identified as "the disabled." It becomes appropriate to think of a disabled person as an individual who is a socially constituted part of us. Both the disabled person and the temporarily able-bodied person can feel a greater sense of self-identity, completeness, interdependence, and meaning in life.

In taking this perspective of autopoiesis, we are involved simultaneously in destroying the perspective of teleology, because we are recognizing that aims or purposes are not features of an organization, either human or nonhuman. Rather, we realize that aims or purposes belong to the domain of our discourse about our actions. We impose our own ideas about aims and purposes on these organizations. Aims and purposes are not separate from us. Maturana and Varela note that our disclosure about any system, as if it were independent of ourselves, reflects our interpretation of this system and the way we ignore its connection within a larger context.

Because we create this idea of purpose ourselves, notions about aim or purpose used by policy analysts to explain culture have no explanatory value by themselves. We act as if they do when we impute purpose to these organizations, but this purpose comes from our interpretation of what we observe; it is not an integral part of the organization itself. Maturana and Varela (1980: 88) note this when they describe teleonomy as only an artifice of description that does not reveal any inherent features of the organization under observation. Teleonomy only points to a pattern that we observe in the operations of the phenomena under study. They write: "This does not preclude their being adequate for the orientation of the listener towards a given domain of thought. . . . Accordingly . . . teleonomy becomes only an artifice of their description which does not reveal any feature of their organization, but which reveals the consistency in the operation within the domain of observation."

The important point to understand is that living systems are purposeless systems, and they only gain the purpose we impute to them. For example, through a process of self-organization or autopoiesis, we create a sense of purpose for ourselves. Similarly, we create our own identity; we learn who we are by the very act of understanding our self-organization.

Over 200 years ago, David Hume made a similar point in critiquing the belief in causality. Hume suggested that causation is a mental construct that we project onto the changing activities we observe. If we use the language of Maturana and Varela, we project onto these phenomena the associated probabilities of mutual occurrence. This suggests that we need to change our understanding of purpose in the world of phenomena to recognize that purpose is not inherent in the nature of any system, human or nonhuman, but rather is a construct created by any observer to explain what actually happens when viewing a system in operation.

This notion that we create our own purpose and draw our own causal links lies deep in Western philosophical tradition. Heidegger, who understands how we have misused the construct of purpose in our Western tradition, teaches us the same lesson when he relates his understanding of production or poiesis. In defining technology and how it is produced, Heidegger says that the object is revealed through a condition of unbounding within the realm of consecration and bestowal. What this means is that an object reveals itself through time because of the way others relate to it or use it. In explaining this phenomenon, Heidegger uses the example of a chalice that is circumscribed as a sacrificial vessel, asserting that circumscribing forms limits to the thing that is produced, but these limits are not finite. The limits serve to reveal the thing. In other words, each object may have its specific form when we perceive it, but then, as we observe it, it can change its form, or the purpose for which it is used, within certain limits that we prescribe. It is these limits that identify the object or individual we observe. Within these limits, objects and individuals are mutable, open to the possibilities for change and, thereby, definition. As Heidegger (1977: 8) explains: "That which gives bounds, that which completes, in this sense is called in Greek *telos*, which is all too often translated as 'aim' or 'purpose,' and so misinterpreted. The *telos* is responsible for what as aspect are together coresponsible for the sacrificial vessel."

In other words, according to the concepts of Maturana and Varela, this passage could be interpreted to say that *telos* or the underlying dynamic within the object or individual is responsible for revealing that object or individual's identity or bringing it into being. Maturana and Varela would say that *telos* occurs through a mutual orientation between interacting objects or individuals that can yield a consensual domain, whereby the interactants agree on the nature and limits of their interaction. Maturana and Varela also suggest that the central feature of human existence is its occurrence in a linguistic cognitive domain, whereby we use language to create our own sense of purpose and identity. Consequently, we are essentially involved in a process of being-in-the-world rather than being-with-the-world. The distinction is that in being-in-the-world, we join in our environment as co-creators of what happens in that world, instead of simply being with others and existing without having any effect on it ourselves.

From this point of view, the disabled, like all organisms, have the ability to shape and change themselves, the temporarily abled, and the environment around them, within certain limits. They are not merely acted upon, but they have the power to act as well. We need to keep this in mind in our relationships with the disabled and in the development of public policy. The basis for evaluating or assessing which set of relationships ought to occur lies in the principle of self-organization, whereby individuals and groups can take it upon themselves to shape their own future. In holding to the principle of self-organization, we then understand policy creation as a domain in which what we communicate about and how we are in relationship to others discloses our boundaries and limits. These boundaries and limits are the preorientations for personal and societal renewal and change, which, in turn, can refigure positions of power and political influence for all members of a community. As Everhart (1979: 420–422) points out, this reconfiguration can happen when researchers use methodologies that generate ideas and information that can actually be used in policy formulation. He further points out that our research usually is not relevant and that policy decisions are made by bargaining and compromising among individuals representing various interest groups. He concludes that the bargaining and compromising should be at the level of data generation and reduced at the level of federal decisions. One could add that not only should information be collected on bargaining among individuals with various interests but also on the limits we have created while defining the social problem in the first place. In the example at hand, research and discussions need to take place among policy analysts and the disabled. In a similar vein, Willner (1980: 91) notes that "the higher up decisions are made, the further they usually are from the people who are supposed to be the ultimate beneficiaries of the program."

How do we create communities that recognize the need and create a context for reconfiguring the positions of power and political influence? In most academic research circles, this question would not be asked because of the belief that power and influence come from the decisions based on research finding rather than being disclosed through the research process. It is assumed that the most important decisions will be made at the national or state levels and will filter down to the community through public policy. However, this assumption bypasses the possibility of permitting a diversity of styles of communities, societies, and cultures to become a reality and, further, to assume responsibility for addressing social problems. As R. Theobald (1981: 106) points out, "in the past, Western and American cultures have striven to reduce the amount of diversity in the society, creating people who were sufficiently alike that they could serve as replaceable parts of a machinelike system." Without diversity, we limit the availability of a wide range of ideas when it is necessary to solve a problem or create a possibility. A question for educators, managers, and policy analysts in professional fields might be, "How can I own and carry out a personal responsibility that moves beyond laws and an advocacy position to one that helps refigure a context in which diversity can exist and in which research, learning, and community-making can possibly take place?" Field-based hermeneutic research is one possibility whereby such a context may be created. The collaborative nature of field-based hermeneutic inquiry is reflective of Margaret Mead's (1977: 146) description of sociocultural anthropologists. She writes that anthropologists can "make a contribution that is distinct from that contribution of other theoretical and applied human science disciplines . . . [when they] study . . . in collaboration with the members of the other group, to produce a product that neither of them could produce alone."

Although the research stance that promotes conversations about vital issues is a necessary condition for critical hermeneutic participatory research, it is not a sufficient condition. Before researchers can engage in research that uses language, conversation, and understanding as a basis for creating a context in which alternatives to specific social and political problems can be formulated and discussed, they need to understand the nature of interpretation, language, and social being. Acting as if these aspects of social science do not much matter and merely taking the philosophy of the rationalistic paradigm and somehow hooking it up with interviews and conversations does not create research marked by integrity. Almost anyone can go out and interview people and even carry on a dialogue. However, it is imperative that researchers understand the style, approach, and activities inherent in field-based hermeneutic research and understand the evolution of some of the ideas that have given impetus to today's discussions about hermeneutics. In social science, there has been the notion for some time that we can pick up a new technique and apply it to research, curriculum, policy, or organization development. However, it is important for researchers and students of research to see that inquiry in a critical hermeneutic tradition is quite a different activity than merely the application of a technique or style of research. In applied hermeneutic research, one needs to bring to the research project an intellectual history, an understanding of implications for following one paradigm as opposed to another, and one's own history. This process goes beyond the application of specific techniques for data collection and analysis and the naive approach to language whereby one assumes that a new world can be named into being.

Our own history sheds light on our present being and helps formulate our future. The same holds true for our research philosophy. We need to understand its development before we can engage in a research process that calls forth changes in both the researcher and the research participants, thus engendering the possibility for living in different communities in educational, academic, social, political, and business contexts.

In Chapter 2 several writers involved in creating the hermeneutic tradition are reviewed to provide a context for critical hermeneutic participatory research.

NOTE

1. I want to draw attention to the danger that is often ignored in social science critique, especially in applied fields, of simply dichotomizing two positions; for example, positivism and hermeneutics. Attention must be given so that a banal version of hermeneutics is not offered as the cure for the ills of positivism and anything that is not positivism is some watered down version of hermeneutics. In alerting us to the dangers of oversimplifying hermeneutics, Ricoeur (1995a: 303) reminds us that "thirty years ago, everything was existentialism. Now, everything that isn't positivism tends to become hermeneutics." He offers an additional caution, which is well suited to applied fields, not to fragment hermeneutics in application so that we end up with myriad "hermeneutics of."

In this chapter I attempt to show that positivism is the dominant paradigm used in applied social sciences in spite of alternative research "tools" to the survey that are adopted, such as interview, dialogues, and transcriptions. In this discussion I also indicate why the positivist paradigm is ill suited for most social science applied research and present the orientation and context for critical hermeneutic applied research.

2

A Tradition of Hermeneutic Inquiry and a Shift to Ontology: Heidegger, Gadamer, Habermas, and Ricoeur

This chapter discusses the work of several writers in the tradition of hermeneutics with a focus on Heidegger's emphasis on ontology, and a brief overview of aspects of Gadamer's, Habermas's and Ricoeur's work to create a context in which field-based hermeneutic research can be thought about and carried out. In an effort to understand the rich history of hermeneutics, the first section is devoted to views of writers in the hermeneutic tradition. Without understanding some of the historical questions and issues that gave shape to today's interest in hermeneutics, we otherwise would develop only a surface understanding of the difference between research within a hermeneutic tradition and the research that most of us have been trained to carry out in social sciences, namely the positivist and analytic tradition. Within a positivist tradition, we came to dichotomize qualitative and quantitative with efforts to convince readers that qualitative research can be valid research. In so doing, discussions focused on concepts, such as measurement, generalizability, validity, reliability, objectivity, subjectivity, and explanation. The discussions, for the most part, remained tied to the positivist train of thought as indicated by the topics selected over the past three or more decades and, in recent years, still discussed (for example, Eisner & Peshkin 1990). In an attempt to discuss other issues related to research, one needs to have a background in different traditions before centering on topics, such as participation, text, narrative, community, history, conversation, and understanding. Certainly, topics in each of the above lists have been discussed in a variety of traditions, but specific topics that direct a discussion often indicate the paradigm one is using to shape discussions. Problems arise when discussions of text, narrative, and other words in a critical hermeneutic tradition are used by people with little in-depth background in an interpretive paradigm. The discussions are superficial and can mislead the reader or researcher in terms of the power and legitimacy of the hermeneutic concepts. I present writers from a hermeneutic tradition, and research herein is viewed as an interpretive personal and moral endeavor.

There is no attempt to explicate or critique the basic principles of any one author's work. Rather, I use various aspects from the work of several authors to reveal a history about understanding and language and in so doing rely on several perspectives. Each author's work embodies a tradition coming from the past into my own tradition, resulting in a present text that projects a future for myself and for the reader. Thus, the study of hermeneutics today is influenced by various traditions. There is always a risk in using labels to determine differences among traditions. Labels either oversimplify or ignore how many writers' work contributes to more than one tradition. In general, in the broad arrangement of hermeneutics, there is the analytic tradition, which includes writers, such as Hintikka, Winch, and von Wright who are interested in logical maps and grammars; hermeneutics and critical theory, with Habermas at the forefront (Ricoeur 1984: 32) refers to Habermas' work as political hermeneutics); the ontological hermeneutics of Gadamer; and the critical hermeneutics of Ricoeur.

I have made judgments about what is important to use from each writer in order to create this book text. Other judgments would be the result of a different understanding of hermeneutics. There will be ideas within the traditions I use that, if dealt with more thoroughly, would not fit into the scope of this book although they are necessary to understand if the reader has a deep interest in ontological and epistemological questions. For example, the ideas of Gadamer and Habermas in their long exchange on the nature of language point to and result in a personal choice, in my opinion, to move beyond the dichotomy of tradition and ideology and to keep working on both an epistemology and an ontology of social science research processes. To spend pages on details of each side of discussions and debates would not serve my purpose, although the differences in some of the discussions are indicated. Today, the debate would take on new dimensions in light of shifts in Habermas's argument. My intent is to provide a philosophical and practical context in which to think about and carry out research in a collaborative fashion that results in furthering an understanding of what it means to do participatory field research in a hermeneutic tradition. Along with this intent is an interest in helping to create conditions for both the researcher and research participants to engage in serious conversation.

An early reference to hermeneutics is found in Aristotle's *Peri Hermeneias* (On interpretation). Aristotle uses the syntax of language as the basis for revealing the nature of things. The Greek verb *hernenuo* means to interpret or explain and the Greek noun *hermeneia* means interpretation or explanation. From an early date in philosophy there was a dynamic among ontology, epistemology, and interpretation — although it is only recently, with Heidegger's work, that questions of ontology have entered our discussions. Later, in the Middle Ages, hermeneutics, as a concerted effort among scholars, had as its purpose interpretation of texts, usually Scriptural texts. Hermeneutics has moved over the centuries from a subsidiary of theology to a general term for the study of understanding.

The question of knowing is a pivotal one in the study of understanding. Immanuel Kant's revolution of thought, in an attack against metaphysics, sought for a unified ideal of knowing. For Kant, both the subject and object take on a clearly defined role in knowing: subject is the knower and object is the reality that is known. In his philosophy, objects are given, in turn, to individual humans — all of whose constitutive nature possess presupposed rules. These *a priori* rules operate synthesizing functions and give spatial and temporal form to human sensations. Kant believed these rules to be the condition for any human experience — ordering sensations into regulative structures that dictate experience. In other words, Kant appealed to an objective world (known) that is independent of a conceptual scheme, one that is the same for all human beings (knower). This transcendental turn, philosophy's Copernican Revolution, was Kant's way of accounting for and grounding the objectivity of knowledge. Just as the sun was the determinant of orbits for the physical universe for Copernicus, Kant situated in transcendental consciousness objective rules for determining all forms of knowing — most critically for him, moral knowledge. Writers and thinkers who succeeded Kant thought erroneous the claim that an objective moral law can be judged and grounded by pure practical reason — reason exemplified in a logical, ahistorical regulatory system. Kant, then, did not succeed in convincing his successors that he had established an objective foundation of morality.

However, Kant did contribute to the development of hermeneutics in that through his writings a new and different usage for the term understanding came into place. Until Kant, understanding was concerned with decoding given meanings and the validity of what was said. With Kant a different usage of the term understanding appeared. Understanding (*Verstand*) pointed to an underlying ability for thought and experience. Our acts of understanding (*verstehen*) were part of our experience and thought and referred to our rationality.

Since Schleiermacher, following Schlegel and Fichte who in the late eighteenth century and early nineteenth century tried to ground hermeneutics directly in understanding, this concept has become the edifice of hermeneutic theory. Interest during this time in hermeneutics was not an attempt to decode a given meaning or reach the proper understanding by determining the validity of a text but rather concern was with the conditions for gleaning the meaning of a text and its various modes of interpretation.

This chapter is divided into four sections, beginning with an overview of selected hermeneutic philosophers. The first section presents a historical background of understanding and interpretation. This section is followed by a focus on the transition from epistemology to ontology in hermeneutic writings. The third section discusses aspects of works of Heidegger, Habermas, Gadamer, and Ricoeur and provides a foundation for field-based hermeneutic research and community. Research carried out in a participatory mode by several people does not necessarily constitute or develop into a community. In fact, rarely does a community formulate during research projects. However, often researchers who go into existing communities have the opportunity to become part of such a community. It is important for researchers to understand the nature of community if they are carrying out research in a participatory mode. Equally important is an orientation on the part of the researcher toward community. The fourth section looks at the role of the researcher and the place of understanding in field-based hermeneutic research. The topics of each of these sections overlap in terms of both specific category and traditions of the writers used in this book.

UNDERSTANDING AND INTERPRETATION

Friedrich Schleiermacher, the father of modern hermeneutics, in the early nineteenth century explained the linguistic dimensions of human understanding. This was a major development in the field of hermeneutics for it opened the door for new foundations to be laid: historical hermeneutics of the nineteenth century and philosophical hermeneutics of the twentieth century.

Schleiermacher's own work brought together ideas from the older schools of hermeneutics and from the German Romantic movement that advanced the notion of a work as a unity and style as the inner form of a work. With these ideas, the further influence of the Romantic concept of art as symbolic, giving rise to the idea of multiple interpretations, and the Kantian position that understanding was part of all thought and experience, the stage was set for modern hermeneutics. The attempts to decode given meaning were replaced with a search for ways to understand and for modes to interpret.

For Schleiermacher, understanding was analogous to speaking, derived from a human being's knowledge of language and an ability to speak. He writes (1977: I.3, I.4.1) that "since the art of speaking and the art of understanding stand in relation to each other, speaking being only the outer side of thinking, hermeneutics is a part of the art of thinking, and is therefore philosophical." He also states: "Speaking is the medium for the communality of thought, and for this reason rhetoric and hermeneutics belong together and both are related to dialectics. Indeed, a person thinks by means of speaking. Thinking matures by means of internal speech, and to that extent speaking is only developed thought. But whenever the thinker finds it necessary to fix what he has thought, there arises the art of speaking, that is the transformation of original internal speaking, and interpretation becomes necessary."

The act of understanding an utterance, spoken or written, involves a dual process: the utterance is part of an interpersonal linguistic system, and also is a moment in the speaker's internal history. Further parallelism follows in that these two sides of understanding correspond to two modes of interpretation. One mode, technical or psychological interpretation, is a divinatory activity that recreates the originality of the speaker — it recreates the creative act. The focus is on the writer. The other mode of interpretation is grammatical and corresponds to the linguistic side of understanding that considers the relation between an utterance or work and the totality of language or literature. Here the focus is on the writer's language. Although these two modes of interpretation have equal status they cannot be carried out at the same time. Either we consider what is common, the language (a grammatical interpretation), or what is peculiar, that is, the subjectivity of the author, the writer's message (a technical interpretation). In other words, either language serves the individuality of the writer — the phenomenological view, or we forget the writer and consider the common language — the structural viewpoint. In the application of both modes — interdependent and circular — it is the technical interpretation that is the proper task of hermeneutics.

The hermeneutic circle was born in the wake of a linguistic turn, holding thought and language to be influenced and shaped by each other. A human being is a linguistic being and is the place where language articulates itself in each speech act. A human being is also an ongoing, evolving mind, and speaking is understood as a moment in one's internal history, or mental life. Mental facts are not independent of language; Schleiermacher believed that speech as mental fact can only be understood as linguistic signification because the primordial nature of language shapes our mind.

With the linguistic element soundly posited in hermeneutic study, Wilhelm von Humboldt in the early 1800s built on Schleiermacher's work and further developed the groundwork for the ontological turn that Heidegger's and Gadamer's work would fully develop in the twentieth century. Humboldt agreed with Schleiermacher that language patterns thought and thought influences language. Schleiermacher and Humbolt viewed language both as a language system and as utterance (discourse) — precursory thoughts of de Saussure's work several generations later.

Humboldt's important addition to hermeneutics was the role of sociability. He held that language was not just a tool for communication to take place but that it was also an imprint of the mind and the world view of the speaker. Further, language for Humboldt was both a process and a product. Language played out its fullest potential when recognized as a process that only occurred in a societal situation. Speaking and understanding for Humboldt correlated to active linguistic competence that took place in the both the speaker and hearer. This is important to understand because we see here that language is not a neutral device that transports meaning from person to person in some transcendental manner. Rather, humans understand each other because they produce and understand utterances according to basic structures of the human mind and the universal structures of the language they share.

As such, active linguistic competence is a cooperative activity that links societies together. The individuals in a society understand themselves in an objective way only when what they utter they hear and recognize as being said by another person. This linguistic competence occurs in both speaker and hearer and therefore is a cooperative activity. Meaning for Humboldt did not take place by some neutral mental activity whereby meaning was transferred from the mind of one speaker to another, such as was purported by Kant's transcendental idealism. Rather, meaning was possible due to a joint effort on the part of the speaker and hearer who both produced and understood speech based on the same underlying principles.

Humboldt set the stage for discussion on objectivity in the human sciences based on his idea that in all cultures there are primary forms of linguistic understanding and communication that underlie individual and social meaning. When one person talks with another, comprehension takes place because of the presupposition of an analog in the other person who is listening and comprehending the speaker and in the phenomena actually understood by the speaker. This pre-understanding relationship between the subject and object anticipates the pre-understanding basis for understanding and interpretation of Heidegger's and Gadamer's work. Humboldt writes that comprehension does not rely solely on the subject or the object but on both at the same time in that it consists of applying a previously present idea to a new specific instance. There is a pre-understanding of the new understanding. This same principle applies to historical understanding as well. The gap between history and the historian, between the subject and the object, is bridged by the same principle. In linguistics, the hearer does not simply abstract from the speaker the meaning of what he says. In history, the historian does not simply let the events over time speak to him. Subject and object in both language and history stand in a pre-acknowledged meaning basis to each other. This relationship exists between the subject and the object because what is manifested in historical events is also active in individual human beings; and for linguistic competence to exist the same principle holds: that which is part of a language system, a grammar, a world view of a society, is also part of the mind of the individual. These pregivens make it possible for people to understand one another and for individuals to understand the spirit of a nation or a community. Humboldt writes of the relationship between a subject and object (1988: 112): "Where two beings are separated by a total gap, no bridge of understanding extends from one to the other; in order to understand one another, they must have, in another sense, already understood one another." In writing this, Humboldt was talking about history, but he applied the same principle to language.

What was called the hermeneutic circle in later generations came from Humboldt's work on the relationship between the subject and object, the parts and the whole of language, and of history. For example, the historian looks at specific events over time and knows that one cannot know all the events, so the historian creatively has to supply the whole to the events in order to make sense of individual events as well as to explain the whole in relation to the part. To understand both parts and whole, they each need to be understood in relation to the other.

These relationships are not unlike relationships that can be established among the researcher and the research participants. The researcher and participants stand together in a working relationship. In these relationships, meaning is created among and for themselves and the community in which they live or work. This creation begins with the reflection of the researcher on the texts created by the discourse with the participants and both the researcher's and the participants' reactions to the texts. The final interpretation (that is, text) is presented by the researcher.

We can see in Heidegger's ontological pre-understanding and in Gadamer's historical pre-understanding the inroads made by Humboldt in hermeneutic understanding. Further on the horizon is the fusion of the interpreter and the text posited by Gadamer and *la chose du texts,* the matter of the text, discussed by Ricoeur.

An important consideration in the history of hermeneutics is Johann Droyson's term *verstehen* (to understand) used to define the nature of research in historical sciences as opposed to the natural sciences. In his work during the last half of the nineteenth century, Droyson developed hermeneutic and historical theories that show how an historian studies the form of events over time. Droyson combined the concept of understanding and investigation whereby the investigative talents of the historian become integrated with the object under investigation. This was Droyson's manner of bridging the subject and object. In other words, his was a "method of investigation," as opposed to the causal explanation of the natural sciences that Bacon perfected.

Droyson's and Humboldt's work provided the bedrock for Wilhelm Dilthey to expand the study of history to the study of human life itself. Dilthey's work sought an epistemological foundation for the human sciences.

It is important to understand that Dilthey used understanding in two ways: one way was from an existential viewpoint, and the other way was from a methodological perspective. In short, what we do is existential; how we explain it is formal or methodological.

The basic assumption in Dilthey's framework rides on the notion that understanding of others is possible in the first place because we express our lives. Philosophically and practically, we place understanding on the everydayness of our lives, and such understandings represent "categories of life." Human beings have an interpretive nature and, therefore, as they live out their everyday lives, they understand. Understanding is not something that comes to them because of something they did, but it is a part of their nature. Understanding is a designated act.

In his second way of using the word understanding, Dilthey articulated the formal activities of the social scientist as understanding, as the scientist placed attention on a specific set of phenomena, such as a school system or a business corporation. This two-edged account of understanding covered the interpretive nature of humans in addition to the form or method needed to legitimatize the epistemological character of research in the human sciences. In both cases of the interpretive activities of the everyday person and the interpretive activities of the social scientist, understanding came from creativity on the part of the individual, an intuitive act, a grasping of the truth at hand. Now social sciences had a method of understanding based on *verstehen* distinguishing it from the causal explanation in the natural sciences. Yet apart from the natural sciences, social sciences still retained the formal aspects of research needed to validate social investigations. In the borrowed term, *verstehen*, from Droyson, Dilthey had the basic principle he needed to attempt to do for the human sciences what Kant had done for the natural sciences in his *Critique of Pure Reason.*

Dilthey theorized that what human scientists understand is always a manifestation, an expressed meaning of life, a life-expression derived from a lived experience. The life-expression is outside or externalized mental attitudes or emotions. Life-expression also means utterance. More than just a verbal expression, however, an utterance carries a broad reference including gesture, voice, movement, visual forms, actions, and attitudes. The lived experience is the source of the life-expression. This source comes from the acts of understanding that we live out, that we manifest. For example, individuals express their movements, actions, and attitudes with the source of the meanings grounded in the lived experience of the individual.

The lived experiences are a middle ground in Dilthey's hermeneutic philosophy. On the one hand, as indicated just above, these acts are manifested in life-expressions, yet on the other hand these acts of understanding are also expressed as a set of meanings independent from the people producing them. Specifically, the lived experiences give life to another set of expressions, those objects that have meaning apart from the individual, objects, such as a legal system or an educational system. Berger and Luckmann (1967) have carried this idea into their analysis of language and reality, giving the term reification to the assigning of life to innate systems, such as schools or organizations. These meaning systems result from the interactions of individuals or works of art. The meanings expressed in the classes of interpretive objects, such as a legal system, provide appropriate expressions that function as a focus for human science research. In other words, the human scientist stands outside the events of history and directs understanding to a particular class of objects. It is in this act of directing attention to a class of events that the human or social scientist's understanding becomes formal and methical. In this way, Dilthey retained the "science" in social science investigations by objectifying the subject and object, thus maintaining the ultimate act in research as one based in an epistemological stance.

The legacy that Dilthey left us was the dichotomy between explanation and understanding — explanation was what took place in the natural sciences and understanding was what took place in the human sciences. Although people *explained* things in their environment, they *understood* other people. Dilthey held the premise that an individual could transpose himself into the mental life of others. Dilthey's reliance on the neo-Kantian tradition gave his philosophy a bottom line of an individual acting in social and historical relations through a psychological mode (compare Makkreel, 1975; Ermarth, 1976). The objection to Dilthey's reasoning is that not all in the social world can be traced to the individual; the objective spirit that Hegel talks about, the spirit of a nation, or an institution cannot be explained by reference to the individual. In his later writings, Dilthey recognized this problem and used Husserl's principle of interconnection by which knowledge of the lifeworld of people is possible. Husserl used this principle because he believed that life externalizes itself in structured manifestations available for others to recognize and understand. He moved from the position of one person understanding another person, or past cultures, by virtue of person's ability to offer signs of his existence, to the position of interpreting an interconnection of works of life. Still the basic philosophical act for Dilthey was a subjective one: individuals interpreting individuals, a psychological enterprise. In the next fifty or so years, hermeneutics was to move the focus of study to an objectivity of life, namely to move the autonomous individual to the autonomous text. This move entailed the objectification of the subject and object in Dilthey's work to the objectification of text in Ricoeur's work. In other words, the question changed from who is the voice of the text to what the text says to the reader.

TRANSITION TO ONTOLOGY

Through the time of Dilthey, hermeneutic inquiry was an epistemological enterprise, drawing its philosophical orientations from the works of Descartes. The Cartesian legacy, referred to as the "Cartesian Anxiety" by Richard Bernstein (1983: 16-25), dominated the historical and social sciences until recently and served as the underpinning for all hermeneutic research, the end goal being to reach the truth of the text. Today there are still many researchers, particularly in education and organizational studies, who rely on the Cartesian legacy for their methodological foundations. However, in view of the impractical results from research grounded in a Cartesian tradition, many social scientists now acknowledge that there is a shift in our thinking about sociocultural data (see Clifford Geertz

[1980]). What follows is a brief overview of the history of this shift from the traditional relation between subject and object, in which the subject is in control of the object, to the subsequent enterprise in which the relationship between the subject and object is an ontological one.

In epistemological hermeneutics, the interpreter, a knowing, objective subject, investigates the text as an object. The investigator is active, whereas the text is the passive object. In this view of hermeneutics, there is the search for the conditions under which, or the rules by which, the subject can know the object, the text. The same view is paralleled by the positivist researcher toward a research population. This position (in research, philosophy, historical inquiry, and so forth) rests on a particular model of understanding viewed in terms of our knowledge of the world. Language is viewed as a means of gaining information, of understanding individual words, not the word itself. Hermeneutics was designed to support and further secure an already accepted understanding of a text, such as the Bible or writings of antiquity. As we saw from the overview of the above writers in the eighteenth and nineteenth centuries, they accepted the same assumption about human beings' relationship to the world as did earlier writers, with the added dynamic of language and then history, thus giving the individual the role of interpreter.

However, if the task is to understand the word itself, and not words of a text, then the task of hermeneutics will move beyond a collection of rules to reading a text that brings renewed and practical meaning to the reader. As Ebeling (1961: 16) writes, "It is not a matter of understanding single words, but of understanding the word itself; not a matter of new means of speech, but of a new coming to speech." This active stance broadens our concept of understanding, moving it from our relationship to a word to our relationship because of a word. In participatory research we move from observing, interviewing, and categorizing our data to living in a relationship with the participants, placing our biases along with theirs in an attempt to hear each other and to work out new contexts in which to live.

We as speaking beings are first and foremost hearing beings, listeners. This imperative of hearing is recorded in Wittgenstein's aphorism: "You can't hear God speak to someone else: you can hear Him only if you are addressed." Understanding in this case then depends on our concept of language, whether we ground language in Being or merely in human thought (see Poeggeler 1972). In critiquing the idea that language is grounded merely in human thought, Heidegger (1959: 157–158) writes that a language dominated by the Cartesian idea of subject and object can do nothing but continue presenting a world that mirrors back man's existing concerns and his current place in history: "[Man] is always thrown back on the paths that he himself has laid out: he becomes mired in his paths, caught in the beaten track, and thus caught . . . excludes himself from being. He turns round and round in his own circle." In other words, one's understanding is only a repeat of what has already been brought to the interpretive process. Nothing new is learned, nothing new can be applied.

To avoid such a circle calls for the role of person as listener rather than spectator because it "is in words and language that things first come into being and are" (1959: 13). The move from epistemology of hermeneutics to ontology of language as the basis for hermeneutic study puts the burden and the privilege on man to learn to listen and to wait. As E. Fuchs (1964: 192, 193) writes, "In the tranquility of faith, where noise is reduced to silence, a voice is heard, the very voice which is of central significance for the texts. The text is itself meant to live." For Gadamer, this aliveness is expressed as understanding — only to be understanding when it is applied. This applicative aspect of Gadamer's work identifies his philosophy as practical. In a text created in hermeneutic participatory research, there is the potential of bringing to the foreground not only new relationships and new understandings but also the traditional meaning and experiences in which the participants we work with linguistically move, namely, the community of memory (Bellah et al. 1985). One of the most important and practical aspects of hermeneutic participatory research is that it relies on building relationships. Because of the fixed time element in field-based research, most often it is impractical to think of the research process as an opportunity to create an actual community. Nevertheless, there can be relationships developed and sustained over time that derive from the initial research project. From such relationships, there can be the building over time of community. The researcher may become a part of the community or the research project itself can be the impetus for renewing or creating community.

The question in practical hermeneutics is how a person comes to understanding. Although Schleiermacher generally is regarded as a classical hermeneutic thinker, his earlier work constitutes a turning point in the history of hermeneutics. Schleiermacher used hermeneutics to achieve an interpretive act quite different from that of supporting an already existing understanding of a text, namely, to make understanding possible in the first place and to initiate understanding in each individual case. The reader, or researcher, plays a radically different role than a subject working on a text or a population. Now the reader or researcher goes beyond his horizons with the act of interpretation. With the work of Heidegger, Gadamer, and Ricoeur ultimately there results a fusion of horizons that takes place when there is a common world in which the horizons of the text fuse with those of the interpreter. This common world can be the basis for possible communities, grounded in common understandings. Field-based hermeneutic research in the truest sense of the term cannot take place without a common world among the participants enabling communication to take place. How this world comes into being is not the result of a protocol, such as interviews, conversations, and data analysis. Rather, it comes into being out of an orientation toward understanding on the part of the researcher and participants; out of the relationships established with conversation partners; and out of a fusion of horizon for each individual.

FOUNDATIONS OF CURRENT HERMENEUTICS FOR PARTICIPATORY RESEARCH

What follows is a brief overview of the ontological thread of thought running through the work of Heidegger, Gadamer, Ricoeur and, in a modified sense, Habermas in their move away from a dependence on analytic epistemology for the foundations of hermeneutics. An important contribution of their work is seen in the avenues they open for the practical application of their philosophy that can be used as a basis in field-based hermeneutic research and the development of community. In such research, the relationship significantly changes from the traditional subject-object relationship between the researcher and the research population found in most social science and educational research. In survey work, interview protocols, and case histories, the researcher is an active subject working on a passive population, manipulating data to follow certain methodologies. Of course, in all approaches toward research, epistemologically directed out of a Cartesian tradition or ontologically directed out of a Heideggerian tradition, data are selected and manipulated to an extent. However, ontologically directed inquiry concerns the relationship between the researcher and the research participants and the active orientation of the researcher toward the research project.

In field-based hermeneutic research, the traditions and understandings of both the researcher and the members of the research population come under consideration. More importantly, they are oriented to work within a common understanding disclosing before us a text that opens new worlds for both researcher and members of the research population. Of course, in inauthentic participatory research lies the possibility of creating a world shaped upon impractical and unjust traditions. The regulatory frame for practical and just decisions resides in each individual in community, revealed and validated through experience and discourse based on moral imperatives. Martin Heidegger set the stage for the move away from traditional concerns of subject and object, this aspect of his work being highly influenced by the work of Edmund Husserl, to an analysis of human beings-in-the world where understanding, a methodological category, is something that is part of human existence.

In *Being and Time* Heidegger investigated the traditional foundations of hermeneutics and showed in this investigation that the question for him was not one of how to understand our existence — posing the question in the traditional object-subject relationship. Rather, the reason for philosophy was to see how understanding *is* being. In other words, his task was nothing less than to provide a pre-ontology of human existence or *Dasein* (being-there). Not since the medieval ages have philosophers placed the question of being as that question in which all other questions may converge.

Understanding, for Heidegger (1962: 143–153), constitutes, along with state-of-mind and discourse, the essence of human beings — the being that understands is *Dasein.* If the essence of human beings is understanding, then we see that the most important aspect of us is an activity, the activity of understanding. To think of a human being primarily as a thing characterized by psychological and physical attributes starts us off on the wrong road. When we believe this about what or who we are, we do research differently, ask different questions, analyze data differently, and exist in a different relationship with the research participants than if we believe that our nature as human beings is foremost about understanding. The point of departure for hermeneutic participatory research is its orientation about our own nature as humans in language and the implications for what can happen when individuals engage others in serious conversation.

Dasein in normal discourse is translated as "existence." When parts of the word *dasein* are separated into *da* and *sein,* "there" and "being" respectively, we can talk about a relationship between time and man's being. Man's being is essentially temporal. The term, "being-there," includes man's conscious, historical existence in the world that by its nature projects into a there beyond its here (1962: 7–8, 12–15, 85–87). (Note: all references to Heidegger's *Being and Time* are to the pagination of the later German editions as indicated in the margins of the 1962 Harper & Row English publication). *Dasein* is conceived as essentially "Being-in-the-world." In this Being there is a unity that overrides the traditional dichotomy of subject and object. In other words, understanding does not arise out of objective or subjective moves. Rather, Heidegger's conception of understanding is meant to capture the object and subject, both the interpreted and the interpreter. Our disclosure of the meaning of anything is a situated understanding, and the structure of *Dasein*, or Being-in-the-world, is distinctively temporal. This temporality is not enduring or lasting but takes meaning in the sense of living in the present (here) from the standpoint of future possibilities projected (there) from the past. The world we live in is a conglomeration of expectations drawn from what came before us. Our personal worlds are inserted within, and shaped by, a broader linguistically and culturally determined weave of relationships, interactions, and possibilities making up an ideology or shared worldview. The interdependence of the world made up of intersubjective networks and our personal world is ontological in nature because the cultural reference points that determine our own identity are reinterpreted in view of our personal expectations and singular circumstances. This reinterpretation is the focal point for current discussions in several applied fields. For example, in education we hear about "recipe knowledge" (Bowers, 1980), "hidden curriculum" (Giroux & Purpel 1983), and "banking in education" (Freire 1985). These examples refer to the inauthenticity of classroom experiences for students who are not encouraged to reinterpret their own traditions and present lives in view of the linguistically, culturally, and politically determined matrix involving them as persons.

Human understanding is circular. It is comprehended in terms of the temporal structure of Being-in-the-world, which is a historical process. In this historical process traditions and communities are maintained and extended over time in different sociopolitical and sociohistorical contexts. Understanding, then, does not take place in a culminating achievement but is an unfolding in time. Understanding is that mode through which possibilities and potential of a person are disclosed, not simply given to someone by someone else.

Heidegger maintains that because humans have an intrinsic concern with Being, human existence possesses an ontological priority, and an analysis of human existence necessarily invokes interpretation. Heidegger tells us that *Dasein's* own state of Being is most often concealed from itself yet is also ontologically closest to itself. This appears to be a contradiction, but Heidegger (1962: 32–35) resolves this dichotomy by contending that human existence embodies as part of its Being, in its ontic constitution, a pre-ontological understanding of self and the world it is in. Heidegger wanted to precisely disclose this pre-understanding nature of *Dasein* in relationship to Being.

Categorizing humans as individual thinking beings, a subject at hand, was not a fundamental or an important consideration for Heidegger. The previously mentioned writers placed great emphasis on the author, the investigator, as a thinking subject, who had authority over a creative work, as well as an important emphasis on the reader, who would read the work and then understand the author. Heidegger, however, did not place his concept of understanding in the subject (the researcher) but rather in a person's Being-in-the-World. For Heidegger, authentic understanding took place when a person came to acknowledge his own essence. It is important for field-based hermeneutic researchers to know who they are and who they are in relationship to those they work with (their biases, prejudices, and interests) in the research project. We can only experience others when we genuinely reflect upon who we are, what we do, and the implications of our actions.

For Heidegger (1962: 38), a phenomenological description, whose *logos* (word, speech, discourse) has the character of *hermeneuein* (to interpret), is identical with interpretation. He believed that Being signified the "business of interpretation." As noted above, Dilthey thought that hermeneutic operations of historians and social scientists were grounded in the basic act of understanding everyday life activities and moved upward to a higher level of interpretation as the historian or social scientist created an overall view of the everyday events over time. Heidegger, however, thought that all acts of understanding, simple or complex, stemmed from a primordial mode of understanding, which is part of *Dasein.* Being discloses itself to *Dasein.* Disclosure is at the center of *Dasein's* primordial understanding. Heidegger (1962: 230) writes that:

The Being of truth is connected primordially with Dasein. And only because Dasein is as constituted by disclosedness (that is, by understanding), can anything like Being be understood; only so is it possible to understand Being.

Being (not entities) is something which "there is" only in so far as truth is. And truth *is* only in so far as and as long as Dasein is. Being and truth "are" equiprimordially.

Heidegger moved from epistemology to ontology, to the foundations of the possibility of human sciences. His effort was spent in critiquing or deconstructing metaphysics. In his hermeneutics of being, however, Heidegger never returned to epistemology, to the structure and methodology of the human sciences. The primary activity of his disclosure was the confrontation with the metaphysical traditions of the West; thus, Heidegger gave to hermeneutics a philosophical meaning. The subject matter of philosophy changed from Husserl's introspectively retrievable phenomena of consciousness with intentional objects to Heidegger's individual who places self-understanding in history. Understanding is possible here only by means of understanding itself by way of interpretation, by disclosing through our language and conversations what it is that is repressed or undisclosed. Heidegger's focus on history gave to his student, Gadamer, the open door to deliver the human sciences from their dependence on method. Gadamer returned to the more ordinary study of hermeneutics — texts, but with works of art as his model. For Gadamer truth is not something we search for but rather something we experience. This gives hermeneutic participatory research a basis for inquiry. Although we may search personally and communally for truth, it affects our lives when we experience it.

For Heidegger, humans are temporal with a focus on the future — we present ourselves toward tomorrow. It is through understanding that the future presents itself to a person — so being and interpretation are the same for Heidegger. *Dasein* projects itself in an act of understanding (the influence of Dilthey is seen here) toward the potential, which becomes, namely, the self-realization. The self-realization is the unfolding of the understanding. Therefore, understanding yields an interpretation. Both Heidegger and Gadamer believe that interpretations are grounded in understanding and are merely the explication of what is already understood. Ricoeur would say that this is only half the journey and that the journey back is when critique and social change can take place — where social action is the text in front of us.

However, it needs to be noted that, although ontology of being marks Heidegger's intellectual journey, inherent in this ontology is critique. For example, his concept of "throwness" (1962: 135, 175) puts a person in a position to live an authentic or inauthentic life. *Dasein* remains in the throw of everyday life and most often does not act out of express consideration but rather simply as a way of being, taken in by benign everydayness. For example, the theses or dissertations of most graduate students in education, business, nursing, and other applied fields are based on survey research or other positivist approaches. In a positivist tradition students do not question or seriously study the implications of their research paradigm; they merely carry out their project in the "normal" manner to meet the requirements for graduation, believing that is the way research is. There is no intellectual or practical *bas relief* to the way research is. By seriously considering the existing research in the positivist and functionalist modes, one can begin to study possibilities in which to carry out other forms of inquiry. It must be noted that Heidegger would not simply suggest that there are alternative kinds of research processes, such as naturalistic inquiry, case studies, experimental, and so forth, and that we could chose one of these "alternatives." Rather he would suggest that we should question the tranquillity that so many university professors exhibit in teaching research methods — question the "throwness" of our way of teaching research. When one, tranquilized and understanding most everything about research, compares oneself with the university researchers, one drifts along toward an alienation in which individual potential is hidden for making meaningful and practical contributions to research in applied fields. For Heidegger (1962: 178) alienation means a closing off from the genuine practical research needed in today's world, its authenticity and possibility.

There are increasing discussions among researchers today (for example, in education) that question the wisdom of carrying out research modeled on Newtonian physics. The questions in these discussions point to a breakdown (Winograd & Flores 1986: 33–36, 145–150) manifested in defensiveness of the traditional way of research, in confusion about qualitative and quantitative research, and in misappropriation of hermeneutic literature. However, the defensiveness, confusion, and misappropriation are *always already* oriented to different or new possibilities. This preorientation simultaneously reveals a conceptual space and tradition of possible research approaches and conceals others. The reason this chapter opens with an overview of some of the writers in the field of hermeneutics is to reveal a context and background that might open possibilities for different avenues for interpretive field-based research. While these pages depict a particular stance toward hermeneutics, they conceal another stance — analytic hermeneutics — that would have generated a different approach to interpretive social science research.

Authenticity on the part of the person carrying out hermeneutic participatory research is a self-conscious event. Researchers do not collect data in conversations and analyze data from a neutral stance. Rather, they are personally involved in the entire research project. A critical aspect of hermeneutic participatory research is reaching new understandings about an issue, problem, or question. The answer, and challenge, is to understand self and others by knowing them in their tradition and culture. For this orientation toward research, Heidegger is the point of departure for thinking about what is important in field-based hermeneutic research. Drawing upon Heidegger (1962: 178), when one understands "the most alien cultures and 'synthesizes' them with one's own," this can lead to a person's "becoming for the first time thoroughly and genuinely enlightened about [him]self." We know who we are and have the opportunity to know others when we think about ourselves in terms of the other.

One of the most important moves made in philosophy was Heidegger's linking the question of understanding not to another person, as Dilthey did, but to being. While Schleiermacher and Dilthey developed an objective enterprise in their hermeneutics, Gadamer holds that what is being interpreted is experienced by us only if our own understanding is involved in the act. This is one way of seeing how the role of the researcher in applied hermeneutic research is a personal role — the use of first person singular in writing up the research is an example of the personal rather than a neutral stance.

Being dwells in language and an individual senses being through language. Heidegger (1971: 5) called "language . . . the house of Being . . . [and] . . . man by virtue of his language dwells within the claim and call of Being." Heidegger goes on to say that the phrase "house of Being . . . gives a hint of the nature of language." Language allows an individual and Being to reside in a relationship with each other. A parallel can be made between Heidegger's notion of language and the notion in this book of field-based hermeneutic research. It can be said that the use of the first person by a researcher gives a hint of the nature of participatory hermeneutic research and that the conversations carried on by the researcher and research participants allow for relationships to develop, providing a common ground for further work and the possibility of developing a community.

The term appropriation is used by Heidegger to describe the nature of the relationship between person and being. A person belongs to language and is appropriated by language. Appropriation is the most simple and inconspicuous of phenomena in which mortals spend their lives. Heidegger writes (1971: 128), "appropriation grants to mortals their abode within their nature, so that they may be capable of being those who speak." Further, appropriation is a law, but not a law that is an ordinance or a norm hanging over our heads telling us what to do, rather it is a "gentle law" *the* law, "because it gathers mortals into the appropriateness of their nature and there holds them" (1971: 128–129). Specifically, (1971: 127) appropriation is "what brings all present and absent beings each into their own, from where they show themselves in what they are, and where they abide according to their kind."

To characterize humans, we can say that we are in relationship with each other even before we make academic, personal, professional, social, or civic overtures to establish relationships. This characterization of human beings is akin to Maturana and Varela's characterization of all living systems as communicative and relational in nature.

Humans dwell in language. Language does not dwell in humans. Language brings worlds into being and, in bringing forth a particular world, the relationships among everything in that world are disclosed. If a person learns to listen, and not only hear, what is already understood, opportunities come into play to open new worlds. The possibility, then, exists for us to live in an appropriation where a person and a world work together, more fully recognizing where one belongs. It is in this recognition that relationships are made evident. From here the building of communities begins, and we can critique our activities. Too often critique does not work because what and who are critiqued belong to different worlds and there is little or no communication to use as a basis for recognizing what in our history we should keep and what we should abandon. If we critique a policy or another's actions without a common recognition of an our world, we are speaking from different traditions, from different worlds. In such a situation, there is perhaps the exchange of words, but meaning escapes the exchange. For critique to become more than the art of merely finding the inconsistencies and injustice in another's argument or premise, there needs to be a context in which we can move from critique to conversation to application. A move from criticism to application is possible if the referent for our discussion is historically grounded, brought to the present, and together refigured to a future.

In Heidegger's work, we acknowledge that inherent in language are the way we are and the way we can become. However, this way of being needs a context, namely, community. A look at aspects of Gadamer's ontological work and Habermas's critical work points to initial considerations of the relationship between being and community. An orientation, on the part of the researcher, toward understanding and community is far more felicitous for field-based hermeneutic research than is an orientation toward mere explanation and the analytic tradition.

BEING AND COMMUNITY

Gadamer

Heidegger's philosophical inquiry grounded language and understanding in ontology of being. Gadamer's philosophy builds on this grounding and broaches application as an integral part of language and understanding. Hermeneutics and praxis are inextricably united in application.

In contrast to Schleiermacher, who held that through understanding one could overcome the distance between the interpreter and the historical phenomena, Gadamer maintains that the nature of understanding is historical. The interpreter's past and his prejudices are a necessary condition of all understanding. Understanding or interpretation, virtually the same for Gadamer, overcomes the strangeness of what is to be understood and transforms the strangeness of the phenomenon into an object of familiarity. Further, understanding is possible because the object to be understood and the person involved in the attempt to understand are in a condition of relatedness transcending historical time. The object and the person (interpreter) are part of what Gadamer calls "effective history." Effective history is made up of an overarching historical and cultural continuum that is the cause of prejudices that function as a necessary condition of historical understanding. Hermeneutic reflection and determination of one's own present life interpretation call for the unfolding of one's "effective-historical consciousness," that is, the effective historical continuum of which one is a part.

The possibility of all understanding for Gadamer rests in language and is historical in nature. The unique capacity of language is to bring about the fusion of horizons of the interpreter, or researcher, and of the historical phenomenon. Specifically, understanding consists of a fusion of horizons in language that is the universal character of understanding. Our language constitutes our world, allowing us to live in a finite but open and changing horizon. The very nature of horizons allows for a hermeneutic fusion. Gadamer (1988 (1965): 269) credits Nietzsche and Husserl for the use of the word horizon, in that they used it to characterize the way in which thought is tied to its finite determination and the nature of the law of the expansion of the range of vision. Specifically, Gadamer writes about horizon:

Every finite presentation has its limitations. We define the concept of "situation" by saying that it represents a standpoint that limits the possibility of vision. Hence an essential part of the concept of situation is the concept of "horizon." The horizon is the range of vision that includes everything that can be seen from a particular vantage point. . . . A person who has no horizon is a man who does not see far enough and hence overvalues what is nearest to him. Contrariwise, to have an horizon means not to be limited to what is nearest, but to be able to see beyond it. . . . The working out of the hermeneutical situation means the achievement of the right horizon of enquiry for the questions evoked by the encounter with tradition.

As noted above, the interpreter and that which he understands are part of a historical and cultural tradition called "effective history." When we come to the hermeneutic participatory research process, within our own tradition, we each have a set of prejudices that are a necessary condition for understanding our project at hand. These prejudices are somewhat like the throwness of Heidegger's philosophy. Neither prejudice nor throwness is prior to consciousness but is its condition. We can never rid ourselves of prejudices because the recognition of some prejudices would entail the dissolving of others. If we had no prejudices, we would have no knowledge. However, we can change our prejudices and therefore our knowledge. In field-based hermeneutic research, it is part of the process for both the researcher and research participants to read the texts created by transcriptions of the conversations. In so doing, we can see more easily our thoughts, our ideas, and our prejudices.

Gadamer (1988: 239–240) writes that prejudice does not mean a false judgment, but rather that we give positive and negative value to long-held opinions. It is important that we are aware of our bias, thus allowing the text to present itself to us in newness and "to assert its own truth against one's own fore-meanings."

When we closely examine and reflect on our research conversation texts, we may be surprised to see who we are. Upon further study and reflection, both the researcher and the participants can place ideas in perspective. The fore-meanings are hidden in everyday conversation where often we are more intent on speaking than on listening, waiting, assessing, and learning.

For Gadamer, both language and history make an integral part of who we are. There is not a method to find the truth; rather we need to expose ourselves to the truth, much the same way we expose ourselves to art. Criteria and guidelines of truth or reason are subsumed in the fusion of horizons, specifically our present horizon of understanding fused with new understanding. Self-consciousness is unattainable, and self-knowledge is a never-ending task. Gadamer so completely rejected the certainty of the Cartesian method that he replaced this certainty with the position that even our own being cannot be perfectly known. This is the case because of the nature of humans; our nature is such that it is not a matter of applying a method to humans to find the truth out about ourselves. Studying ourselves and others by using a method is not only insufficient but also misleading.

The meaning of a work or text for Gadamer takes on life through an interpreter's explications, which are "nothing but the concretion of meaning itself." In field-based hermeneutic research, both the participants and researcher are interpreters. The final text of the research project at hand, of course, is the responsibility of the researcher. The research work is part of a historical continuum, no matter what the research question is, and it is through the knowledge of history that we come to know ourselves and others. This knowledge is sustained by a speech community and is linguistic in nature. This knowledge is possible because what is said by a speaker (each person speaking in the research project) directs the dia-logue, and the speaker fades away. The dialogue, which we are, and our prior understanding become the "matter" of the text and stands apart from the speaker and the text as such. This matter of the text stands ready to be used by community members of a school to develop curriculum or a com-munity of managers in a corporate setting to design corporate policy. These communities in a school, a business, local neighborhoods, or spe-cific locales of a country are intentional communities whereby the mem-bers have common vision and purposes enacted in practices that bring forth new narratives that give direction to our relationships and our lives.

When we use Gadamer's philosophy as the basis for hermeneutic par-ticipatory research, our work leaves us with a hermeneutic consciousness. However, we are then open to Habermas's question on whether or not the truth-oriented approach of Gadamer's hermeneutics could also provide a critical consciousness. Although there is not an attempt here to resolve the differences between these two writers, I suggest what I believe are their strengths in terms of using parts of their philosophies as guidelines for field-based hermeneutic research. In using Habermas's work as a basis for research, the analysis of data takes on a more critical stance than does research following Gadamer's work, which draws the researcher to look closely at history and language. Along with Gadamer's concepts of histo-ry and language, the concept of fusion of horizons is useful in both data collection and analysis. In Habermas's work, the framework for social science is formed by examination of modernity developed by his concepts of rationality and communication.

Habermas

Habermas disagrees with Gadamer's idea of dialogue being that which we are because of a major principle in Habermas's work — the idea of anticipation. Communication for Habermas does not proceed from us, an intrinsic aspect of our history. Rather he calls upon a regulative ideal of communication that is the guide for our interactions with others. This guide is from our future, not from our past. The human sciences for Gadamer are essential and renew cultural heritage in the historical pre-sent; they are always of tradition reinterpreted and reinvented, but nonetheless always of tradition.

Inquiry for Habermas rests in three spheres governed by three respec-tive interests: technical, practical, and emancipatory. His first interest is referred to now as purposive-rational action; the second and third inter-ests, practical and emancipatory, are now referred to as communicative (symbolic) action. In his earlier writings (see *Knowledge and Human Interests* [1971]), these interests assumed a quasi-transcendental status. He revised his position in *The Theory of Communicative Action* (1984, 1989) to claim that communicative action is based in language, specifically in speech act theory, rather than in individuated subjects. Habermas's original concern was one of determining how autonomous subjects can be related. This proved problematic. Philosophically and practically, in any attempt to understand human society, community, and history, there is always a problem if the issue is to connect person A with person B. This approach stems from the basic intellectual grammar housed in Newtonian mechanics, which claims a linear relationship between A and B. The point, however, is to look at the relationship between A and B. It is in this relationship that humans find identity and a framework in which to ask questions and pose answers. Thus, in his revised position, Habermas is able to move from his emphasis on a subject to the orientation between a speaker and a hearer — the starting point being their orientation to reaching mutual understanding. Accordingly, his theory now has a dialogical bent rather than a monological one. Habermas focuses on language-in-use, that is, our speech. His framework and foundation for a social theory is in the form of a theory of action established through communication. Inherent in communicative action is human rationality. Habermas (1984: 397) reasons: "If we assume that the human species maintains itself through the socially coordinated activities of its members and that this coordination is established through communication — and in certain spheres of life, through communication aimed at reaching agreement — then the reproduction of the species *also* requires satisfying the conditions of a rationality inherent in communicative action." Habermas claims that our ability to communicate reveals that those who learn to speak a language learn more than merely the ability to produce grammatical sentences. In speaking, we relate to the world about us, to others, and to ourselves. In each of these spheres, we are always making claims, explicitly or implicitly, concerning the validity of the truth of what we are saying in relation to the objective world; concerning the sincerity of our own intentions; and concerning the legitimacy of our values and norms in our social world.

Habermas's idea of a speaker and hearer reaching understanding relies on the use of reasons to attain intersubjective recognition for validity claims that can be criticized. Claims on prepositional truth or effective ways to carry out a plan can be criticized and defended with reasons and arguments, as can the claims that an utterance is an authentic or sincere assertion of one's experiences, as well as the claims that an action is right or appropriate in a certain normative situation. In each of these three domains it is possible to reach agreement of claims through argument and reflection without resorting to force or manipulation. Specifically, Habermas (1984: 17–18) explains that "the rationality proper to the communicative practice of everyday life points to the practice of argumentation as a court of appeal that makes it possible to continue communicative action with other means when disagreement can no longer be headed off by everyday routines and yet is not to be settled by the direct or strategic use of force."

Communicative rationality is an aspect of learning. Learning in Habermas's framework is associated with critique, recognizing our mistakes, and choosing another way of thinking about or doing something. This is far different from the sequential model on which most of our curricular or management activities depend for form and content. If learning is carried on at a reflective critical level, forms of reasoning and argumentation may be learned by others and developed within a cultural and political tradition. They could be actualized in specific education plans, management programs, legal systems, and other conformations of social phenomena. In this way, communicative action could critically connect individuals and their lifeworld structures to traditions and present day social institutions. Habermas realizes that before this connection can yield a social theory, empirical and theoretical work of research programs based on these ideas would need to be carried out over time. Habermas (1984: xl) describes the development of his plan for the basis of his work in the following way:

The concept of communicative action is developed . . . which provides access to three intertwined topic complexes; first, a concept of communicative rationality that is sufficiently skeptical in its development but is nevertheless resistant to cognitive-instrumental abridgments of reason; second, a two-level concept of society that connects the "lifeworld" and "system" paradigms in more than a rhetorical fashion; and finally, a theory of modernity that explains the type of social pathologies that are today becoming increasingly visible, by way of the assumption that communicatively structured domains of life are being subordinated to the imperatives of autonomous, formally organized systems of action. Thus the theory of communicative action is intended to make possible a conceptualization of the social-life context that is tailored to the paradoxes of modernity.

This process of investigation for Habermas begins with the recognition that an interpretive stance, hermeneutic in nature, provides the only access possible for social inquiry. He traces his history, though in part disclaiming it, when he writes (1984: 107) that, for Heidegger, understanding is characterized ontologically as a basic feature of human existence, although for Gadamer reaching understanding is a basic feature of historical life. Habermas goes on to say that, although it is not at all his intention to follow systematically this approach, the methodological (as opposed to the ontological) academic discussions concerning social science foundations have ended up with similar results. He cites Giddens (1976: 135) to support this point:

The generation of descriptions of acts of everyday actors is not incidental to social life as ongoing *Praxis* but is absolutely integral to its production and inseparable from it, since the characterization of what others do, and more narrowly their intentions and reasons for what they do, is what makes possible the intersubjectivity through which the transfer of communicative intent is realized. It is in these terms that *verstehen* must be regarded: not as a special method of entry to the social world peculiar to the social sciences, but as the ontological condition of human society as it is produced and reproduced by its members.

Habermas describes this ontological condition as processes of reaching understanding through which and in which the object domain is antecedently constituted prior to a theoretical understanding of it. When a social scientist studies an object domain, he meets a symbolically pre-structured reality in the process of constituting the same object domain. The inner logic of this domain resides in generative rules according to which the social scientist and other people who appear in the domain produce the social context of life together, directly or indirectly. Habermas (1984: 108) explains that the "object domain of the social sciences encompasses everything that falls under the description 'element of a lifeworld'." He clarifies intuitively what this expression means "by reference to those symbolic objects that we produce in speaking and acting, beginning with immediate expressions (such as speech acts, purposive activities, and cooperative actions), through the sedimentations of these expressions (such as texts, traditions, documents, works of art, theories, object of material culture, goods, techniques, and so on), to the indirectly generated configurations (such as institutions, social systems, and personality structures)."

Above, Habermas describes the ontological nature of elucidating a socio-cultural lifeworld. Recourse to such a world is possible only through the fundamental concepts of speech and action, which, in turn, entail both the social science researcher and the research participants belonging to the lifeworld under investigation.

This belonging is an ontological condition of members of social life and is of critical importance in the study of community. In a sense, we are in community as we are in speech and action. Traditionally, community has meant small groups cohering because of a common purpose or tradition. Although these considerations characterize aspects of community, a more fundamental characterization is one of people belonging to each other in an ontological sense. Community, like understanding, is ontological and universal. The sedimentations and configurations in which community expresses itself are various but we are always part of a community, always already in a community. Recognition of this aspect of our nature highlights the study of ourselves in a more immediate sense than does an emphasis on our past or future, yet community is birthed in our tradition and anticipated in our future.

Although Gadamer relies on interpretation for understanding, Habermas's use of hermeneutics plays a different role. He says social science begins with an interpretive turn. All we know about ourselves and others is interpreted by us.

Habermas posits that the critical sciences are distinct from the technical, or empirical, as well as from the historical-hermeneutic, or practical, sciences. The critical sciences reflect human beings having an emancipatory interest in securing freedom from underlying forces and conditions of distorted communication. This interest is rooted in man's capacity to act rationally, to reason upon reflection, and to make decisions based on knowledge, regulations, and needs. Man's self-formative process can be a process in which history is made with will and consciousness. Habermas posits that history made with will and consciousness happens when rational capacities of human beings are released and a self-knowledge is generated through self-reflection. Self-reflection can guide individuals in the recognition of conditions that dominate and repress people.

The impetus to achieve self-understanding and autonomy of action in our lives reflects our interest in reason. This interest is an emancipatory interest. Habermas believes that systematically distorted communication and thinly legitimized repression are seen as the conditions for claiming an emancipatory interest, because there would be nothing to be emancipated from unless there is institutionalized domination in our social lives. The emancipatory interest is the guiding interest of critical social research. Inherent in this interest is the act of self-knowledge through self-reflection, thereby bringing to consciousness structures of systematically distorted communication, which in turn can be revealed and specified. Specifically, in developing countries the act of self-knowledge through reflection on the part of the researcher and the participants, who are often in policy-making positions, can begin to create a context in which appropriate decisions can be made.

It should be noted that it is not the case that, merely because someone engages in self-reflection, there will emerge a correct and just policy. This is Bowers' (1987: 126–136) point when he writes that reflection is not enough to establish the basis for legitimate social action. Although reflection is important, memory and the mediating structures of community and education in addition play a critical role in learning how to live in and shape a society.

Habermas is aware of the importance of self and writes in the Introduction to *Theory and Practice* (1973: 22–24) that in a rational reconstruction of our society, there is a place for self-knowledge to emerge. In other words, self-knowledge takes hold in a process of rational reconstruction, which in turn is uncovered in discourse. This type of discourse is unfolded in Habermas's theory of communicative action. Although the theory of communicative action, and its implications for theory and praxis, is in an unfinished state and is part of Habermas's ongoing social theory that has been the subject of discussion, debate, and revision (see Thompson & Held 1982; Bernstein 1983) there are aspects of it that are highly useful both methodologically and theoretically for hermeneutic participatory research. Following immediately are comments on the nature of the individual and his role in discourse as posited by Habermas. The purpose of presenting these comments is to work toward establishing a working relationship between being and community that can help field-based hermeneutic research make a positive difference in the lives of the people who are part of a research project or who would be affected by similar issues. A longer-range, positive difference would be a contribution toward a social science where empirical data on international understanding, justice, morality, liberty, and freedom find a forum that speaks to both the individual and the public. The work here and the examples in the last chapter may point to a direction and to some of the issues and conversations that could become part of such a social science from a hermeneutic participatory perspective.

Habermas does not attempt in his theory of communicative action to present a detailed outline or plan for the perfect society or community. Bernstein (1983: 192) writes that such a "reading of Habermas (for which he is in part responsible) seriously misunderstands his primary point that in the genuine plurality of forms of life rooted in their unique tradition, we can detect a gentle but obstinate, although seldom redeemed, claim to reason, a claim to reason that points to the possibility of the argumentative redemption of validity claims through mutual dialogue and discourse."

For Habermas the principle of communicative action, and a concomitant communicative rationality, is not an arbitrary ideal nor is it put into place by authority. He asserts that this principle, characterized by the validity claims of comprehensibility, shared knowledge, trust, and shared values, is "always already" implicitly raised in action oriented to reaching understanding. Habermas (1979: 97) writes, "These universal claims [just listed] . . . are set in the general structures of possible communication. In these validity claims communication theory can locate a gentle but obstinate, a never silent although seldom redeemed claim to reason, a claim that must be recognized *de facto* whenever and wherever there is to be consensual action." Consensual action based on participants who comprehend one another, share knowledge, trust one another, and share values is the action that could be the procedural, not specific, basis for developing and evaluating our policies, our forms of education, or our communities. If, in turn, reason were redeemed in this action, we would have a backdrop by which to look at our own communities and reasonableness in social life. Habermas (1982: 226–228), in a reply to his critics on communicative reason, explains that his commentators miss the point when they stylize communicative rationality into a *particular* value, for or against which one can take sides. A theory of communicative rationality is a structural and a procedural phenomenon. In a specific case the actual shape of a life history is embedded in its own unique narrative and would not be in a position to be judged by a theory. Speaking and hearing participants who want to arrive at a decision concerning contested validity-claims of norms (practical discourse) or statements (theoretical discourse), Habermas (1982: 227) posits, "cannot avoid having recourse, intuitively, to foundations that can be explained with the help of the concept of communicative rationality. Participants in discourse do not have to come first to an agreement about this foundation; indeed, a decision for the rationality inherent in linguistic understanding is not even possible. In communicative rationality we are always already oriented to these validity-claims, on the intersubjective recognition of which possible consensus depends."

Habermas goes on to explain that "communicative reason operates in history as an avenging force." Communicative reason as a theory is identified as structural and conceptualized as procedural, and, therefore, is not in danger of overstating its claims precisely because it is formalized. In other words, a theory such as this can rely on standards for the critique of social relations that may be morally questionable and not legitimate. However, this theory never was intended for, nor is it capable of, judging the value of competing forms of life. Specifically, Habermas (1982: 227–228) writes that theory:

Cannot judge the value of competing forms of life. To be sure, the concept of communicative rationality does contain a utopian perspective; in the structures of undamaged intersubjectivity can be found a necessary condition for individuals reaching an understanding among themselves without coercion, as well as for the identity of an individual coming to an understanding with himself or herself without force. However, this perspective comprises *only* formal determinations of the commmunicative infrastructure of *possible* forms of life and life-histories; it does not extend to the concrete shape of an exemplary life-form or a paradigmatic life-history. Actual forms of life and actual life-histories are embedded in unique traditions.

One way we can relativize our lives, and, hence, gain perspective is to juxtapose actual forms of life and life histories with possible forms of life and life histories. In a culture that is weak on historical reference points (Bowers, 1987: 18), we don't have many opportunities to look back on how lives were lived out, the morals that shaped the lives, and the communities that sustained our work and personal lives. We have been curiously committed to change as a sign of progress rather than a comparison with what we used to do. This is not to say that what was done in the past is what we should do now. Our past grounds us and gives us perspective. As Ricoeur (in Kearney 1984: 21) writes, "I believe we must have a sense of the meaningfulness of the past if our projections into the future are to be more than empty utopias." It is in conversations with speakers oriented to reaching understanding that the validity claims are raised — that there is the possibility of telling our story of the past and evaluating it. A conversation is an event during which several things may take place: we evaluate ourselves and others, we tell and retell our story, we see the past, and we pose possibilities for the future. Although the formal determinations of the communicative infrastructure of *possible* forms of life cannot evaluate our actual forms of life, they provide a backdrop for our conversations out of which come stories that preserve "the meaning that is behind us so that we can have meaning before us" (Ricoeur in Kearney 1984: 22).

Ricoeur

The preservation of meaning is possible for Ricoeur because just as there is in the individual a generic communicative competence, preceding and independent of a particular utterance, so in a particular utterance, which becomes a written work, a text, there is both a participation and an independence, or distanciation, from the particular references that the participants in conversation actually had in mind. Speakers and hearers intentionally participate in discourse. What they say, after it is said, no longer belongs to either the speaker or the hearer. It has, in a sense, a life of its own. In addition, the meaning of what is said no longer belongs to the intentionality of the conversants but rather to the being of the utterance itself (Ricoeur 1982: 131–162). This preservation of meaning enables us to communicate at a distance, a distance created over time. Ricoeur (1982: 62) refers to this enduring meaning as the "matter of the text," which belongs to neither the author nor the reader.

Ricoeur wants to place the text on a footing whereby the readers can distinguish between legitimate and illegitimate interpretations. Although Gadamer gives insight to the critical role that language and tradition play in our lives and in our interpretations of our texts, he virtually ignores method in the social sciences. Ricoeur (1974: 15) maintains that the important task of hermeneutics is to offer the possibility of "a true arbitration among the absolutist claims of each of the interpretations."

The problems of textual interpretation are related to the problems of meaning and language. Discussions on the philosophy of meaning and language, in brief summary, reveal a dynamic principle in view of Dilthey's critique of his teacher Schleiermacher. For Schleiermacher, understanding was embedded in language and man's linguistic nature. Dilthey, however, established understanding as a methodological construct with its origin in the process of human life. At this time in the history of hermeneutics, understanding was moving with life itself. The individual, for Dilthey, was fundamentally singular and acted in the stream of life's events uniting history and hermeneutics. In his efforts to make history intelligible and to retain the scientific dimension to social science, Dilthey stayed on the side of epistemology, that is method, rather than ontology, which is being. In his day, the model of intelligibility was grounded in the context of natural sciences. Ricoeur (1982: 49) recalls and comments on the question posed by Dilthey: "how is historical knowledge possible? or more generally, how are the human sciences possible? This question brings us to the threshold of the great opposition which runs throughout Dilthey's work, the opposition between the explanation of nature and the understanding of history. The opposition is heavy with consequences for hermeneutics, which is thereby severed from naturalistic explanation and thrown back into the sphere of psychological intuition." The neo-Kantian position is that the pivot of all human sciences is the individual. This position directed Dilthey to the presupposition that an individual has the innate ability to transpose himself into the mental life of others. Therefore, Dilthey searched for the distinctive features of understanding in the sphere of psychology. In so doing, the unfolding of the text was, for Dilthey, toward the author. To understand a text, according to Dilthey, one has to understand what is in the mind of the author. If the author is living, presumably one can ask the writer first hand. Still, if I ask any of the writers of the examples in Chapter 3 of this book what was meant, the meaning might not be the same as when the author created the text — time and experience change each of us. If it is a historical text that one is studying, one has to take part, at a distance, in the transference of another mental life. In the social sciences, the term *verstehen* is often used to refer to the method employed to empathize, intuit, or grasp the meaning behind the data, to understand what is in the mind of another.

In Heidegger's work the question of how to gain access to another mind was solved when the question changed from how one communicates with another to one of how a person is in the world. The philosophical pivot changed from individual to understanding. Heidegger posits understanding not as a way of knowing but as a mode of being. Ricoeur (1982: 54) points out the nature of this difference in the questions he asks: "instead of asking 'how do we know?', it will be asked 'what is the mode of being of that being who exists only in understanding'?" Essentially, one question is a question of method and the other is a question of truth.

In Gadamer's work, as mentioned above, the truth was favored over the method. Still, in Gadamer's work, we see the importance of tradition, which implies a distance that, in turn, suggests the possibility of analysis and critique. This critique, however, cannot be governed merely by an interest distinct from our interpretation of history. As Habermas writes, the unique traditions and life histories are not to be judged by an arbitrary ideal. Habermas argues that the potential to make judgments resides in our claims to reason manifested through an appropriate orientation and through communicative acts.

Ricoeur posits that there is an ideal that can serve as the basis for critiquing the present and for evaluating our individual lives. This ideal obtains its essence and significance from the creative appropriation of the past. The medium of appropriation is historical and social texts.

A text is not dependent on speakers, as noted above, or an author for meaning. Objective meaning of a text is not derived from grasping the subjective intentions of the author as suggested by Dilthey. Rather, as Ricoeur argues, the text holds the meaning, not the author or speakers in the discourse that became text. For Ricoeur, both explanation and understanding make up the revelatory process of discovering meaning. It is possible to understand a text apart from the author because there is something beyond intentions of an individual. This "beyond" is the matter of text that gives the interpreter the reservoir of phenomena needed for the exegesis.

The exegesis consists of explanation and understanding. To explain a text brings out the structure of the text. To understand the meaning of the text calls for interpretation — an appropriation *here* and *now* of the intention of the text. Specifically, Ricoeur (1982: 162) writes that "to interpret is to follow the path of thought opened up by the text, to place oneself *en route* towards the *orient* of the text. We are invited by this remark to correct our initial concept of interpretation and to search — beyond a subjective process of interpretation as an act *on* the text — for an objective process of interpretation which would be the act *of* the text."

The referential dimension of a text unfolded in the process of interpretation is an important aspect of Ricoeur's philosophy for field-based hermeneutic research. The referential dimension points to future possibilities and alternatives for our social problems and requires creativity on the part of the interpreter(s) to imagine new possibilities and configurations of social life and policy. In hermeneutic participatory research, discussion about future possibilities is made possible by what the text points to. What is appropriated is the matter of the text. This text, created from transcriptions of previous conversations, provides a proposed world that the reader or researcher could inhabit and in which they could project possibilities.

Based on these ideas, hermeneutics cannot be defined as an inquiry into the hidden meanings beneath a text ferreted out through the grasping of psychological intentions of an author or speaker. Rather, hermeneutics is described by Ricoeur (1982: 112) "as the explication of the being-in-the-world displayed by the text. What is to be interpreted in the text is a proposed world which I could inhabit and in which I could project my ownmost possibilities."

The text is a meaningful entity only when thought of as a whole. However, what one interpretation of a text means, or proposes, may be in conflict with another interpretation. This can be resolved to an extent by a process of argumentation and debate. In such debate intentions of the author, or researcher who writes the text, may be relevant but are not decisive.

For example, a researcher generates data in conversations about the taken-for-granted understandings of our actions, social structures that hold action in place, and about the everyday events in our lives. These conversations are transcribed into text, thereby drawing a configuration from a mediation between diverse events, such as goals, motives, prejudgements, and a text as a whole.

The plot of the story is refigured, which opens new guidelines for action. In studying the text and in returning the text and preliminary analysis to the participants for further discussion, additional meaning or possibilities are disclosed — thus, refiguration. These meanings, in turn, are subject to further critique and interpretation. The analysis of the whole text — the transcribed conversations plus the debate and critique of them — includes guidelines for application of new ideas and alternative policies and programs. These guidelines applied in real classrooms, in actual corporate settings, and in other arenas provide an opportunity to test them. In addition, their application also provides the medium in which practice, reflection, critique, and further refiguration can take place.

The above scenario is a broad and preliminary association of Ricoeur's theory of *Time and Narrative*, volumes I, II, and III (1984, 1985, 1988) with hermeneutic participatory research. Ricoeur's concept of mimesis described as "imitating human action in a poetic way" (1982: 179) is a creative act that "makes humans' actions appear higher than they are in reality" (1981: 181). This appearance is the matter and referent of the text.

The relationship between time and narrative is linked to a threefold mimesis. Ricoeur (1984: 52) believes his ideas on mimesis give him the opportunity to test his basic hypothesis "that between the activity of narrating a story and the temporal character of human experience there exists a correlation that is not merely accidental but that presents a transcultural form of necessity. To put it another way, *time becomes human to the extent that it is articulated through a narrative mode, and narrative attains its full meaning when it becomes a condition of temporal existence.*" In other words, when we tell a story we capture time. One can say that in a story our past and future belong to us, and the story we have to write (or read) only takes on meaning in the here and now of our lives.

The threefold mimesis refers to three domains: a past, a present mediating act, and a future. Ricoeur uses the subscripts $_{1,2,3}$ to identify the different mimesises. Mimesis$_1$ is the world of everyday action already characterized by a meaningful conceptual network that makes narrative possible. To represent human action we first need to pre-understand what human acting is in its various forms. In other words, something has to exist before it can be configured. Human action is distinguished from physical movement. Physical movements do not have morals, goals, or motives, nor do they rest in circumstances. Moreover, to act is to act with another, taking the form of competition, cooperation, or struggle. Mimesis$_1$ creates the prefigured life, our traditions, assumptions, goals, and motives, whereas mimesis$_2$ imitates the configured life. The temporal dimension of the configured life mimesis$_2$ is a mediating function. Ricoeur here is interested in learning what precedes our stories and follows them.

Ricoeur (1984: 64–70) explains that mimesis$_2$ mediates between the world we already have come to — already characterized by certain actions and cultural artifacts — and the world we can imagine ourselves inhabiting. As described earlier (Herda 1997a: 62) and applied to organizations:

When we look at the already figured world, the take-for-granted world in mimesis$_1$ we connect this to the new world we want to live in, mimesis$_3$, we see ourselves in different capacities; we see a self enlarged by the appropriation of a proposed world which interpretation unfolds. Here the organizational member (or the reader in literary terms) makes his or her own that which was once foreign or alien. In this act, we have to overcome cultural distance and historical alienation that separates us from the proposed text—the proposed organization.

How do we move from pre-understandings to new understandings? How do we overcome the pre-understandings that separate us from the new understandings that carry us beyond the current order of our lives, in organizations, schools, and communities? We reflect and distance ourselves from our prejudices and pre-understandings. Although we belong to history, we also can distance ourselves from it when it is in narrative form. We can read and reflect. To make sense of the story requires an act of emplotment, which transforms and configures a manifold of events, the unity of a temporal whole. To grasp a whole is to make a judgment about new intentions, new meanings. Discourse fixed in writing provides the window on the reference (matter) of the text that "distances itself from everyday reality, aiming toward being as power-to-be" (Ricoeur 1982: 94). The researcher and participants here are interested not in what is behind the text, but what the text opens for future possibilities.

Mimesis$_3$ represents an act of reading in the relationship between time and narrative. It is an intersection of the text and the reader and creates an imaginary world we might inhabit. If we cannot imagine how our organizations could improve, we can never live in a world different from the current conditions. Narrative at the stage of mimesis$_3$ has its full meaning when it is restored to the time of action and suffering. Ricoeur (1984: 70–71) writes that "this stage corresponds to what H.-G. Gadamer, in his philosophical hermeneutics, calls 'application.' . . . I shall say that mimesis$_3$ marks the intersection of the world of the text and the world of the hearer or reader; the intersection, therefore of the world configured by the poem [text] and the world wherein real action occurs and unfolds its specific temporality." In participatory research in a hermeneutic tradition, this third stage is an appropriation of the text in addition to an opening up of possible new actions in the real worlds of our lives and organizations.

Below are the three descriptions of mimesis adapted from Herda (1997a: 61–63) with reference to the place each domain might take in an organization. The researcher or organizational consultant mediates the theory of time and narrative with social organizational texts and organizational members. This mediating function allows the transformative power of retelling a story to be used to draw out meaning from a diversity of people, events, histories, and ideas of our futures and, further, from our work to draw out a new quality of time. Using the same phrase Ricoeur (1984: 64) uses to describe the relationship between literature and human action, the act of applying literary analysis to organizational or community analysis, "opens the kingdom of the *as if.*" Whether it is a matter of analyzing a literary text or an organizational text,[1] there is only the *as if* to serve as the referent for our work.

Mimesis₁ — What we walk into when entering an organization
    a world already *figured*
    a world always informed by cultural artifacts
    practical understanding that poses and addresses questions: when, what, why, and for or against whom
    a preconception in place: norms for judging behavior, implying success, failure

Mimesis₂ — How we make sense of our present organizational life
    is a narrative *configured*
    mediates between individual events and a story taken as a whole
    brings about a synthesis of heterogeneous factors, such as people, goals, interactions, circumstances, unexpected results
    brings forth an emplotment that extracts a new configuration which invokes judgment
    results in a new configuration and quality of time

Mimesis₃ — The organization we want to become
    a *refigured* action
    an act of reading, appropriating with indirect reference back to what is already present and to what is being configured
    an imaginary world we might inhabit
    an intersection of organization (text) and member (reader)
    different ways of acting and being (ethics and ontology)
                         (Herda 1997a: 61–63)

All three stages of mimesis are creative acts and are interrelated. Although action is present in all three stages, it is most important at mimesis$_3$. At this stage we imagine ourselves acting and inhabiting a world with indirect reference to the world in mimesis$_1$. There is a new possibility for living our lives and carrying out our policies when we critique our taken-for-granted world. The researcher is responsible for leading the act of mediation between mimesis$_1$ and mimesis$_3$ to come to new understandings. Not often does the researcher have the opportunity to work with participants in testing out the new ideas in the everyday world unless the project continues for some time. When this happens, mimesis$_3$ is more crucially referenced in the world of ethics because how we act and what we do entails judgment and choice. Although judgments and choices are part of reflection on the pre-understood worlds we live in and are also a part of the mediation function, the world of ethics finds a more immediate presence in our actions in the classroom, the boardroom, and the village — all of which draw us in or out of community.

When the question at hand is, for example, what is the good curriculum, the appropriate policy, or the right management program, the application and evaluation of the curriculum, policy, or program are a trial and test of the interpretation. In practice and reflection, individuals collaboratively can determine the value and meaning of lives affected by programs. If the programs promote living our lives guided by wisdom rather than expedience, and if they promote everyday activities shaped by a care and concern for others rather than by a spirit of independence and autonomy, then a better interpretation of a text may ultimately and in retrospect be determined. In our interpretations, the worlds we propose cannot be finally evaluated with intellectual technology, such as the determination of a text's structure or a text's understanding. Rather, the ultimate evaluation comes in whether or not we live our lives in moral, economic, and political community — a community that is always on its way.

THE POSITION OF THE RESEARCHER
IN HERMENEUTIC INQUIRY

Social science researchers are limited in their understanding of a lifeworld in much the same way that an ordinary layperson is, because they are similarly members of the society or situation they want to describe. To understand a world, they must participate in that society or situation. Participation requires belonging. Investigating speech acts and actions as aspects of a lifeworld is one way to contribute to a clearer understanding of the dynamics involved. As Habermas writes (1984: 108),

Speech acts and action are the unclarified fundamental concepts to which we have recourse when we wish to elucidate, even in a preliminary way, what it is to belong to, to be an element of a socio-cultural lifeworld. The problem of *verstehen* is of methodological importance in the humanities and social sciences primarily because the scientists cannot gain access to a symbolically prestructured reality through *observation* alone, and because *understanding meaning* [Sinnverstehen] cannot be methodologically brought under control in the same way as can observation in the course of experimentation. The social scientist basically has no other access to the lifeworld than does the social-scientific layman. He must already belong in a certain way to the lifeworld whose elements he wishes to describe. In order to describe them, he must understand them; in order to understand them he must be able in principle to participate in their production; and participation supposes that one belongs . . . this circumstance prohibits the interpreter from separating questions of meaning and questions of validity in such a way as to secure for the understanding of meaning a purely descriptive character.

Questions of meaning and questions of validity relate both to what our actions mean and what actions we actually can participate in as researchers studying social problems. As researchers, we need to examine the commitments we express when we converse with each together as researchers and as members of the polity. Further, we need to examine these actions for the additional possibilities they suggest to us that may be different from the actions in which we are now engaged. This realization, in turn, leads us to ask these questions: What actions are possible to carry out? What will be the domain in which we can carry out these activities? What determines the right actions to take? Moreover, what rational capacity will contain us in our efforts? If we use subjective or practical reason as a basis for mediating our current status and a future world, we often fall into the trap of telling others what they ought to do. Relying on analytic or objective reasoning neutralizes anything that appears meaningful. Habermas (1996) offers an alternative reasoning in his study on the mediation between facts and norms and maintains that communicative reason, which is grounded in language, bridges worlds that historically have been divided. Habermas (1996: 3–4) argues that "what makes communicative reason possible is the linguistic medium through which interactions are woven together and forms of life are structured."

The critical point from the above reference for participatory research is that reason and language are intimately connected. The language Habermas refers to is the everyday language of both the researcher and the members of the research population. To use this language for data collection and for analysis rather than an artificial language, such as logic or math, requires an interpretive turn on the part of the researcher, especially researchers in applied fields, such as education and business. Until now, for the most part, the social science tradition in the United States has been influenced by the Anglo-American academic tradition and generally never takes seriously the gap between our thoughts and the world we live in, and has never recognized that this gap presents us with real and practical problems. Once we recognize this situation and try to close the gap, we need to consider new responsibilities and commitments. When we do think of this gap, we tend to fill it with generalizations that ensure the mind's collusion with the world we attempt to describe.

The alternative stance that researchers can take is one in which researchers can begin to engage in conversations that speak of "we" rather than "you" or "they." As researchers, we can realize that we are not separate from the world of action and the social environment under study.

Pitkin (1972: 328) speaks of this quality of belonging when she asserts that political theorists need to recognize their links with others. She writes that: "such a theorist would speak about the political situation of 'we,' not 'you' or 'they.' And saying 'we' here is an invitation, not a command; the theorist is into the royal 'we.'" If we take seriously the act of reinterpreting our world and our past activities, we will realize that we are not simply reviewing and analyzing past theories, policies, or assuming the role of an advocate. Rather, we are using our knowledge and understandings to aid in shaping the future and interpreting the past with a preorientation that we will use this knowledge to create new possibilities for the future.

Because the researcher, or interpreter, must engage in the participants' discourse, the interpreter's attitude partly defines the research stance. Geertz (1983: 70) believes that true understanding can be attained through "thick description" — a simultaneous view of local detail and global structure — and says that researchers must have an accepting attitude. As he warns, "normal capacities for ego effacement are essential if we expect people to tolerate our intrusions and accept us as persons worth talking to."

Like Geertz, Habermas (1984: 120) believes the researcher must maintain a stance of acceptance, but he describes acceptance as more than just attitude. He requires that the researcher implicitly take "a position on the validity claims that those immediately involved in communicative action connect with their utterances." When researchers share commitment with participants to change the context, and hence often the problems, our virtual participation with the polity members allows us to move within their structures of possible understanding. Sharing these structures is important because they provide the critical means for going beyond an established consensus, for revising it, renewing it, or reconfiguring it.

During the interviewing process in critical hermeneutical research, it is not so much a matter of an interview as it is a conversation. Discussed in Chapter 3 is Gadamer's work on play and conversation, which fits in with one of Habermas's validity claims — truthfulness. In a participatory research conversation, it is important to have this process provide opportunities for participants to develop competence in raising universal validity claims; it is also important that the process allows for the emergence of critique, reinterpretation, and creation of new meanings that can inform current activities and future possibilities.

Although the researcher needs to participate in the participant's structures of possible understanding, it is also necessary to take responsibility for saying it right, so to speak, rather than relying on a preconceived form. Treating discourse as an event understood as meaning, the researcher discerns the coherence among the parts of the text, so that a thick description is an appropriation of the univocity constructed by the "Saying" (Heidegger, 1971) or "poetry . . . a voice out of the voices that surround it" (Geertz 1983: 117). As such, the method used in this investigation is a process, mediated by language, in which meaning is appropriated by the participants (including the researcher) through activities of discernment called interpretation (Ricoeur 1982: 44).

One advantage of this method of investigation is that interpretation can provide a description of our knowledge, of the satisfactory and unsatisfactory conditions we have created normatively, while revealing false criteria that can be examined critically and acted upon. The purpose of participatory research is to create conditions whereby people can engage in discourse so that truth can be recognized and new realities can be brought into being.

It is possible to learn a deeper understanding of one's own interests and purposes as another's interpretation is revealed. The process is not characterized as consensus-building, such as that which happens in political debate where conflicting interests are compromised, but rather as discourse that involves engagement and transformations.

In Habermas's model of communicative action, participants are enabled by their ability to communicate understandable meaning among themselves. Underlying this ability is a supposition that rational consensus will be recognized in the light of "common standards" that inform the final decision (Habermas 1984: 113). In the model of communicative action the speakers and hearers need to be *oriented toward reaching an understanding*. In using the model of communicative competence as one important consideration in guiding conversations in participatory research, we see that research is not a neutral activity. The researcher is engaged in the research process with a commitment and an orientation toward collaboration. The transformatory potential of participatory research is present within language and actions of the researcher and the participants. Transformation, however, is further determined by the tradition and environment in which we live. The rightness or wrongness of the transformations can only be evaluated ultimately with insight and wisdom over time.

Chapter 3 gives an overview, with discussion and examples, of the protocol for participatory research within a hermeneutic tradition. Although language, dialogue, communication, and mutuality are respected in hermeneutic participatory research, the person carrying out the research has the responsibility for deciding what the overall nature of the project should be. There is no exact method that one follows. People looking for the method miss the point of hermeneutic inquiry. In addition, although the researcher strives to establish a relationship based on equity, there are points where equity cannot be sought, especially in the directives and learning aspects of participatory research. There are times when the participant is at the controls because of the lack of knowledge on the part of the researcher. At other times, the researcher is at the helm because of experiences brought to the research. In carrying out hermeneutic field work, the serious researcher will have struggled with the ideas and concepts in the hermeneutic tradition. Coming to a research project from an ontological genesis rather than an epistemological one requires reflection, risk, and, for the most part, a change in orientation toward research and social reality in general. Often the lay person we invite to participate in our research project has not experienced such paradigmatic shifts. The burden is on the researcher to understand this and assume responsibilities of a teacher, in a broad sense. The researcher is in the position to ask questions not usually asked by the participants. In order that the questions might have meaning, the participants must trust the researcher and have confidence that the research process they are a part of is a meaningful activity. Bowers' (1987: 157) point in discussing a related subject of teacher/student relationships fits aptly here: the balance between bonding and teaching that leads to critical reflection, and between continuity and renewal will be the real test of our ability to bring research home to meaningful communication and new and better worlds in which to live.

NOTE

1.   An earlier reference to looking at organizations as texts was made by William Foster (1986: 200). In his critique on leadership in applied educational

settings, he writes that "A literary model suggests that we might better understand administration if we looked at schools as texts being written, rather than as social structure needing scientific delineation and definition."

3

A Research Orientation and Protocol in Participatory Hermeneutic Inquiry: Creation and Analysis of Text in Field Research with Implications for Learning and Community

This chapter discusses the theoretical and practical aspects of field-based hermeneutic inquiry in addition to research examples. On the surface, there appears to be a significant difference in complexity between the concepts presented in the theoretical discussions and the activities presented below in the discussion on research protocol. In research classes of most applied fields, the emphasis is on methods, not the tradition or theory behind the methods. Often we are interested in knowing how to do research. When we ask how to do something, we expect to be answered by someone telling us the steps involved. To a certain extent, this type of answer applies to the question: "How does one carry out field-based research in a hermeneutic tradition rather than in a positivist or analytical tradition?" However, although there are steps involved, they need to be thought of more as guidelines. Upon reflection, a more thorough answer would require that one must also consider the theory behind the steps. Both the protocol and the theory behind aspects of the guidelines are presented below. Each researcher has to create a personal way to do hermeneutic participatory research. One could read the protocol discussion and decide to carry out a project following the guidelines with a very limited understanding of hermeneutics. This would be a research project of sorts. However, in integrating hermeneutic theory in our orientation toward the research project, in the fieldwork, and in the analysis, one comes out with a different project than if one followed the protocol within a positivistic or analytical framework or with no theoretical grounding.

In field-based hermeneutic research, the object is to create collaboratively a text that allows us to carry out the integrative act of reading, interpreting, and critiquing our understandings. This act is a grounding for our actions. The medium of this collaborative act is language. Phelps (1988: 192) notes that in Ricoeur's philosophy, "language takes the place of the perceptual world of objects, so that texts become the objects from which human existence is indirectly understood or 'read'." A text (discourse fixed by writing [Ricoeur 1982: 143]) and social actions that are recorded (Herda 1990: 51) allow us to recognize, challenge, and evaluate our worlds of action as well as to envision new, possible worlds. Objectivity comes when we distance ourselves from the text. Practical use of our research data comes from the act of appropriating new ideas and ways of being from the text. In other words, in hermeneutic field-based research the focus is on our distanciation from and our appropriation of the text.

Our research analysis discloses a possible world from the text — the medium in which we understand ourselves. From a position of self-understanding in relationship to others we build new possibilities into everyday life. The most critical manifestations of such possibilities are the new personal and professional communities we build. Community-building in schools, corporations, hospitals, or wherever does not come about just from conversing about common interests and mutual problems but rather from developing relationships based on trust, which is what it takes for a community to be more than a social enclave. A second manifestation is the learning that takes place. Learning here goes beyond knowing what one does not want or like, or inferring that a critical stance is an informed stance. Learning here entails entering into moral and political discourse with a historical understanding of the issues at hand; risking part of one's tradition and current prejudices; and, at times, seeing the importance of community and social cohesiveness over specific desires of the individual.

To make analysis possible, the spoken word in conversation needs to be fixed in a text. Ricoeur suggests that this fixation, distanciation, takes place in four ways: the separation of the event of saying from the meaning of what is said; the separation of the intentions of the speakers from the meaning of the text; the referential difference between spoken and written discourse; and the world that the text when read points to. The task remains to make the text one's own after the act of distanciation takes place. This subsequent act is one of appropriation — an interpretive event. The discussion of distanciation and appropriation sets the context in which field-based research in a hermeneutic tradition takes place. The role of the researcher is far different than a collector of data, an expert, a neutral player, or a partner in a dialogue. The researcher's orientation toward the research event as a whole gives opportunity for one to become a different person than before the research took place. It sets the researcher in a reflective and imaginary mode, thus opening new ways to think about the social problems that drew one to research in the first place.

To create the text in field-based hermeneutic research, conversations among the researcher and participants are transcribed. It is in conversations on issues that are important to both the researcher and the participants that both the ideas of the researcher and participants find an open forum. Further, it is in the narrative text of these conversations that one may see new possible worlds in which to live. Such possibilities are engendered by our imaginations as we read and study the text, turn it back to the participants, and re-read it integrating their comments.

In discussions with research participants, the conversation's reference is determined by our ability to indicate a common reality among the interlocutors, a here and now. However, when the conversations and subsequent discussions become transcribed and fixed as a text, a social science fiction, the question of reference of the text takes on a different meaning. Here we find the core of this approach to social research.

As indicated in Chapter 2, many philosophers have searched for the referent in psychological, historical, or sociocultural venues. However, the reference of the text could not be established in these places because writing is not solely a step of inscribing a conversation, whether or not it has to do with culture, intentions, or history. As Ricoeur (1982: 91) explains, "Writing is not simply a matter of the material fixation of discourse; for fixation is the condition of a much more fundamental phenomenon, that of the autonomy of the text. . . . What the text signifies no longer coincides with what the author meant; verbal meaning and mental meaning have different destinies." The written text transcends its own conditions and opens itself to unlimited readings. Each reading is situated in a different context. In Ricoeur's (1982: 91) words, "the work *decontextualizes* itself, from the sociological as well as the psychological point of view, and is able to *recontextualize* itself differently in the act of reading. It follows that the mediation of the text cannot be treated as an extension of the dialogical situation. For in dialogue, the *vis-a-vis* of discourse is given in advance by the setting itself; with writing, the original addressee is transcended. The work itself creates an audience, which potentially includes anyone who can read."

The moment we fix our discourse in writing, we distance ourselves from the text. The meaning contained in the text is rendered autonomous from the researcher who created it, the original situation in which the conversation took place, and the original persons for whom the text was written. What we say contains the seeds of what the said will be — the said being rescued in a text by the fixation of the saying. As indicated above, the referential function of discourse is the ability to point to a reality common for the speakers, although the reality may shift and be understood differently in the course of a conversation. In abolishing this first order reference in conversation, we arrive at the second order reference in writing, which reaches a type of being-in-the-world unfolded in front of the written text. Now, the reference of the text is the "matter of the text" as Gadamer calls it, or the "world of the text (or world of the work)" as Ricoeur refers to it. What Ricoeur appropriates from the text is a proposed world. This world is not behind the text or beneath the text as hidden (or even overt) intentions of an author, rather the world is in front of the text, as that matter that the text unfolds or reveals. In Ricoeur's (1982: 143) words:

Ultimately, what I appropriate is a proposed world. [This world] is not *behind* the text, as a hidden intention would be, but *in front of* it, as that which the work unfolds, discovers, reveals. Henceforth, to understand is to *understand oneself in front of the text.* It is not a question of imposing upon the text our finite capacity of understanding, but of exposing ourselves to the text and receiving from it an enlarged self, which would be the proposed existence corresponding in the most suitable way to the world proposed.

The mode of being opened up by the world of the text corresponds also to a researcher's own mode of being, both of which reside in one's imagination. We stand as new beings in front of a text that holds the possibility of new worlds for us to live in. Our social reality redescribed in a text is raised to fiction when it moves from our conversations to a written document. No written document replicates social reality exactly and, as such, is a fiction that carries with it the possibility of new selves and new worlds being proposed and appropriated. In short, we distance ourselves from our initial research conversations when transcriptions are made. We appropriate new possible worlds from readings of a text.

Although the conversations and the creation of the text are critical to research, there are other aspects that form a general protocol that one can follow to identify a topic, set up an inquiry process, and collect and analyze data. In so doing, one can create a text that remains open for further reflection and action. Hermeneutic research protocol reflects a moral and historical stance. I believe that the creation of a text is one way we can see where we have been, where we are, and what future we might envision and project. Although the intentions of both the researcher and the research participant are vitally important in the research act, just as important are three other aspects of the research project: the community developed in our working together, the understandings that emerge from our collaborative work, and the idea of a future that we can work toward.

In addition to portraying the moral and historical implications of hermeneutic research, this chapter offers a comparative research schema to help further understand the myriad differences between analytic and hermeneutic research. Further, I present a ten-point process for a research protocol, followed by more in-depth discussion of the most pertinent topics in participatory hermeneutic research. The topics are focus of research project, background of researcher, research categories, research questions, field testing conversation questions, participant selection, entree to research site, researcher and participant collaboration, research conversations, and creation and analysis of text. Research carried out in the critical hermeneutic vein can have important implications for learning in the individual's life and in organizational communities. This learning brings people together and renders us contemporaries with similar goals. Learning and community is the final section of this chapter.

A MORAL AND HISTORICAL STANCE

The guidelines for field-based hermeneutic research are not to be thought of as a systematic procedure. Rather, these guidelines are suggestions that can serve as an idea of how to carry out one form of participatory research, one that is grounded in a particular philosophy, namely, critical hermeneutics. As with any research process, the choice of the problem, the entree, the ethics, and protocol in collecting and analyzing data all point to serious responsibilities that a researcher must assume in social science inquiry. Most specifically, in hermeneutic field-based research, the researcher needs to assume the stance that both the research participants and the researcher have the opportunity to see mistakes and wrong doings in their present and in their past. To document mistakes requires taking an ethical or moral position on an issue. The data do not speak for themselves. Our history and our present voices speak for us, and, thus, our language can either mask or reveal problems that traditionally have been skirted or left unspoken.

For example, in the frantic drive to include the latest technology, or a more direct route to economic competitiveness, a developing nation in designing social or economic programs may ignore the critical importance of historical reflection and actual needs of local people. If traditions and culture were taken seriously and conversations were carried out with local people who are the technology and policy recipients, developers could come to understand with the recipients what part of their history is worth keeping, what part needs to be left behind, and which technologies are appropriate. Although researcher and developers may not be in a position to know or understand enough to make appropriate value judgments, we need to attempt to converse with other nationalities, or with our colleagues and neighbors, to sort out both our history and theirs. Each partner in a conversation comes with prejudgments or, as Gadamer writes, prejudices. For Gadamer (1988: 240) prejudice "means a judgment that is given before all the elements that determine a situation have been finally examined . . . does not mean a false judgment, but it is part of the idea that it can have a positive and a negative value."

Gadamer speaks methodologically about conscious understanding, which calls for our concern with the tyranny of hidden prejudices. It is the tyranny of hidden prejudices, Gadamer (1988: 239) writes, "that makes us deaf to the language that speaks to us in tradition." We have to frame our current idea of science, economic development, research methodology, or whatever it is we are investigating within the understanding of tradition and put it at risk, to frame it in a critical perspective. This, writes Gadamer (1988: 239), "is the concrete form of the historical consciousness that is involved in understanding." Influenced by the writers in the enlightenment period, we have come to think of prejudice as something negative. Thus, "the fundamental prejudice of the enlightenment is the prejudice against prejudice itself, which deprives tradition of its power." However, if we bring to light our prejudices and fuse our present horizon of understanding with new understandings from histories of others, we are in a better position to make policy, curriculum, and management decisions.

I want to emphasize that the researcher who approaches a research problem within a critical hermeneutic tradition is no less immune to inappropriate biases and negative prejudices than the researcher who carries out more traditional kinds of research. The biases and prejudices are different between empirical analytic and empirical hermeneutic research, but not absent in one or the other approach. In research that holds to logical or analytical tenets, there exist techniques to validate and make the research act reliable. In critical hermeneutic research, our attempt is to bring biases out into the open, not to technically reduce or control them. The ahistorical and apolitical stance, which is assumed in the logical empirical and analytical traditions by virtue of the research mode, changes the nature of the data so that biases are hidden. However, all researchers come to the research field with much to place at risk and with a responsibility to be as clear as possible to see what they and others hold as true, right, and just. Upon such recognition, it is incumbent on us to place these ideas in an historical and moral perspective. We can do this in conversation with others. It is in conversation and in the creation of texts that we can open and examine our histories and decide what about them we need today and what we would be better without.

All research approaches are ideologically grounded. How we choose to examine the grounding, or if we choose to do so, is an individual matter. Yet, in the preparation of graduate students, there is a major problem because of the lack of awareness that choices exist. Graduate students are not taught enough history, literature, or philosophy to be able to frame and risk their own ideologies. Often they come to the research field with a canned idea of what research is and fulfill the traditional research requirements in applied fields, such as education, nursing, and business, without understanding the basic assumptions on which the research process rests. The attempt to carry out research from a neutral perspective has produced in researchers the habits of looking at patterns and conventions and describing them — statistically, ethnographically, or with other research modes — without reference to time, temporality, or the meaning of the story they tell. There is little, if any, recognition of the importance of collaborative reflection on the research findings in relation to the larger educational, business, or other applied professional community that extends beyond the conventions or patterns revealed in the research. How do we change our actions as researchers within the broader professional community so that our findings may take on significance in our own lives and in the lives of the participants?

There are at least two answers to this question. The first is to change our notion of action from one grounded in behaviorism (based on the concept of stimulus evoking a response) to one grounded in moral decisions, and the second is to change our idea of professional identity. Rather than thinking that professional identity is derived from individuals in relationship *to* other professionals in a field sanctioned by gatekeepers to the journals and professional meetings, we can think of our professional lives as a calling to work with our colleagues by collaborating with others *in* an extended community of education, business, or other applied fields. Although the gatekeepers of any profession are important in that they keep before us the present paradigm, thus giving us a context in which to critique our profession, they should not be the only ones to set the criteria by which we determine whether someone is successful. Professional relationships and actions in the field are just as important as what is published or what is said in a paper presented at professional meetings. What Bellah and his colleagues (1985: 293) write about university education can also be applied to the university professor: "When education becomes an instrument for individual careerism, it cannot provide either personal meaning or civic culture." The distinction between a career and a profession rests in the difference between fulfilling ritualistic requirements for advancement, on one hand, and, on the other hand, carrying out collaborative action that exhibits moral transformation and civic responsibility.

A similar distinction lies in the difference between a research protocol that on one hand calls for members of a research population to serve as subjects who are to be protected from the researcher — protection ensured by committee approval of the research and a legal document — and, on the other hand, a protocol that engages, within a tradition, both researcher and research participants in a collaborative, interpretative, and moral act. In hermeneutic research, the relationship between the researcher and members of the research population is based on both parties being oriented toward reaching understanding (Habermas 1979). To partake in an act of hermeneutic field-based research is a reflection of approval. One does not engage in a genuine conversation with another person unless both parties approve of such an activity.

COMPARATIVE RESEARCH SCHEMA

At this point it is helpful to view comparatively some differences between research in an analytic tradition and research in a hermeneutic tradition (see Table 3.1). As in any comparative scheme these comparisons are not equal nor do these columns adequately or completely represent either approach to research. The purpose of this scheme is to give an idea of the nature of the ideology that informs our approaches to research. In reading this comparison, there needs to be recognition of the ontological difference between the two schools of thought for research implications. Although there is a technical difference, one could carry out a research project using many of the ideas on the right hand side of the scheme and still think with the ideology that informs the left hand side of the scheme. To understand the nature and implication of critical hermeneutic field-based research requires a shift in how we think about the nature of language, society, and human beings.

A PROTOCOL FOR FIELD-BASED
HERMENEUTIC RESEARCH

The research protocol is a guideline for thinking about and designing a field-based hermeneutic inquiry project. Each of the examples characterizes one individual's interpretation of research in an hermeneutic tradition. Because language, understanding, and culture are constantly changing, it is not possible to offer a closed set of instructions, or steps, that determines the way one *does* hermeneutic participatory research. It is not so much a matter of *doing* hermeneutic participatory research as it is a way of *being* a researcher. Knowing how to do hermeneutic participatory research does not mean knowing how to use particular techniques to design questions, create response sheets, and collect and analyze data. Rather, it means learning about language, listening, and understanding. Specifically, it entails an awareness of the critical difference between research that uses tools and techniques and research that lives in language. Tools for research are those that are picked up and used and then put away for future use — the survey, the statistical tests, the scoring sheets. However, a hermeneutic researcher understands that we live in a world that is already familiar to us and to the participants, that we cannot pick up language, use it, and then put it down until the next research project. We never find ourselves trying to designate a world that we discovered while we were collecting data. Rather, in the hermeneutic participatory research process we acquire a familiarity and acquaintance with the world itself — the world of vocational education, teacher socialization, adult education, multinational management education, or the world of whatever — and how such a world confronts us. As a researcher, one's charge is not to merely represent or symbolize human affairs by creating a contrived correspondence between propositions and what they denote. Rather, the charge is more inclusive — to disclose a world of our participants and ourselves.

Several considerations shape and give specific meaning to a hermeneutic participatory research project. In discussing a general protocol for hermeneutic participatory research, several topics have a bearing on the research process: the focus of a research project, the research categories, questions and conversations, the selection of participants, data collection and analysis (distanciation and appropriation), and learning and community. These topics are discussed below. Prior to this discussion, a brief process outline is presented of what attitudes, orientations, and activities are involved in field-based hermeneutic research. Although this outline covers the general process of the research activities, it is not the heart of

TABLE 3.1
Comparative Research Schema

Dimension of Comparison		
Paradigm	analytic logical empirical	critical hermeneutic empirical
Research goal	prediction and control	understanding; fusion of horizons
Social reality	represented by discrete functional/structural units that add up to a whole	persons actively participate in creating reality; whole/part relationships over time
Language	a representative tool of reality	an integral mode of being
Participants	discrete subjects	community of interpreters
Objective	mirror reality	live out reality
Orientation	is	ought
Rationality	based on linear thinking, symbolic logic	embedded in critique, actions, moral imperatives
Examples of approaches	survey, experiment, case study, ethnography, statistical analysis, structured/semi-structured interview	critical interpretive ethnography, discourse/conversation, explication of social texts
Speaking to/with others	interview, dialogue	discourse, conversation

Source of validity	rigor sanctioned by method	legitimacy sanctioned by values, agreement
Research stance	neutral, "all things equal" reduce/control for prejudice, bias	value-laden, evaluative, acknowledge/risk prejudice, bias
Research referent	quantified data; descriptive, naturalistic data	narrative text, social action
Role of researcher	independent from research subjects	engagement with research participants
Permission to conduct research	outside committee sanctions research project, legal implications	research based on agreement and personal relationships, legal and moral implications
Voice orientation	impersonal, third person	interpersonal, first person
Time orientation	time stops, study is atemporal; replication of study	step into living present, past/present/future ongoing, distanciation, appropriation
Focus	diagnosis, intervention	interpretation, understanding, application
Application	techne, skill, technical know-how	phronesis, wisdom, ethical know-how
Action	strategic	communicative

participatory research in a hermeneutic tradition. If one pursues this research direction but does not have an understanding of the theory of language in critical hermeneutics, the analysis falls short of an interpretative and a creative act. What follows this process outline is an in-depth discussion of several issues touched upon immediately below.

Hermeneutic Field Inquiry Process

Each person who carries out a field-based research project in a hermeneutic tradition needs to formulate and design a personal protocol. No one else can do it for the researcher. It is not a methodology, but a research process and an orientation that directs and shapes the inquiry. The following suggestions represent a composite of several years of experience and many projects that may serve as the beginning outline for thinking about participatory research in this tradition.

Make a Commitment to Field Inquiry in a Hermeneutic Tradition

Perhaps this is the most critical element in this kind of participatory research. Research in this mode calls for substantial effort. It requires belief in your ideas in addition to a willingness to find out that you may be wrong about some dearly held prejudices. It also requires academic and intellectual preparation.

Choose a Topic or Research Focus Carefully

The topic or focus one chooses is one the researcher must live with for many months and should be grounded in a deep interest.

Carry Out a Review of Literature and Develop a Theoretical Framework

A review of literature provides a background of the topic. Examples used in the discussions below reflect topics of interest of the specific researchers. In the original work from which these examples are taken, each writer provided a review of literature on the specific topic. An additional review on critical hermeneutics was carried out as well. This second review provided a background for an analysis of the conversation texts.

Develop Initial Categories

Categories are derived from the literature, one's interests, one's experiences, or a combination. Categories serve as general parameters for the research inquiry and data collection process as well as themes for the analysis. Categories may change as the research progresses.

Propose Initial Questions and Conversation Guidelines

Although it seems a simple thing to do, asking the right question or creating a context in which a conversation can be carried out is far from simple. Such an activity needs practice.

Pilot the Questions and Conversation Guidelines

From the pilot or field testing of the question, the researchers can determine how well they ask questions or how well they can engage people in conversation. This experience also creates a practical opportunity to see whether the categories provide the right emphases for the research.

Select Participants and Develop Entree

Participant selection and entree require that the researcher has a thorough background in the issue at hand. People often are not interested in talking to someone unless the person doing the inviting gives the impression that he is knowledgeable and sincere about the project. Timing, flexibility, and persistence are often the critical elements needed to gain entree into a particular setting. Other settings, however, are very inviting, with people eager to talk with someone who shares their concerns and interests. It is important to explain to participants that they play a major role in developing the knowledge and understanding that are a part of the research project. When possible, it brings more ownership to the overall project to engage the participants in the identification of the problem as well as the choice of questions or points for discussion. In each project there will be formal participants invited to participate in the study. However, there may also be informal conversations carried out with people who are not part of the formal arrangements. Often these conversations are very informative. They also serve often to introduce the researcher to other potential participants.

Data Collection and Text Creation

Data are collected through conversations that are recorded and transcribed. The transcription is a text — the fixation of our conversation in writing. This is an act of distanciation, a distancing ourselves from our conversations. Optimally, there are at least two conversations with a participant. The transcription of the first conversation is sent to each participant with an overview of the conversation and a short comment by the researcher. Receiving this text is an opportunity for the participant to review and reflect on what was said. Any changes the participants want to make in the text need to be honored. If they request an anonymous conversation, that too, of course, needs to be honored.

The second conversation begins with the text for further conversation about the issue under investigation. Often the second or even third conversation is carried out in a more creative mode whereby the conversants can think about ways to address the problem. Time and distance constraints make it difficult, but when it is possible for several of the participants to gather for a conversation, such conversations often prove to be insightful and exciting. The conversants share not only the conversation experience with the researcher but also share to a certain extent knowledge about the issue at hand. This is the case because often the researcher teaches and learns in the course of the research interview conversation. Further, researcher and participants learn from each other.

An important source of data is the personal log or journal kept by the researcher. This document is the life-source of the data collection process for in it goes the hopes, fears, questions, ideas, humor, observations, and comments of the researcher. A forthright and well-documented log will show remarkable changes over time in the researcher's understanding of both the process and the theory.

Data Analysis

Analysis is a creative and imaginative act. In data analysis the researcher appropriates a proposed world from the text. When we expose ourselves to a text, we come away from it different than we were before. As Ricoeur (1982: 53) says, "The text must be unfolded, no longer towards its author but towards its imminent sense and towards the world which it opens up and discloses." Implications in such research are often two-fold: the researcher sees the world differently than before the research, and implications are manifest for looking at the everyday problems differently. The following is a helpful sequence in setting the stage for analysis:

Fix the discourse by transcribing taped conversations. It is best if the researcher does this rather than a machine or another person because in hearing the conversation one lives through the conversation experience again from a different perspective. Listening to one conversation brings to bear nuances, further ideas, and the opportunity for reflection on what was said. Reading all the conversation transcriptions allows one to develop an overview of the issue at hand and begin appropriating a new world from the text.

Pull out significant statements, develop themes, and place them within categories. If the original categories are not appropriate, change the category that does not serve any purpose. There are times when it is impossible to anticipate which categories will maintain or surface throughout the research.

Substantiate the themes or important ideas with quotes from the conversation transcripts or with observational data as well as data from the researcher's log. In using participants' quotes, try to remain as close as possible to the original language. How much editing is appropriate is a question about which the researcher needs to think and decide. For example, when the language of the text is a second language for the participant, it may be appropriate to modify grammar, if it is incorrect, for clarification.

Examine the themes to determine what they mean in light of the theoretical framework of critical hermeneutics. There should be a certain amount of spontaneity among the themes, quotes from the conversations, and the theory. Also, bring in data, noted below, from observations, outside document study, and personal log.

Provide opportunity for continued discussion and conversations with participants using the developing text when appropriate. Note any changes requested by participants or any further ideas they may contribute.

Set a context for the written discussion.

In developing the text, discuss groupings of themes and sub-themes within each category in light of the theory and the problem at hand. Often themes may fit into more than one of the categories. If so, indicate this in the discussion, bringing in more than one dimension to the theme or grouping of themes.

Discuss the research problem at a theoretical level, thus implementing a further practical use for critical hermeneutics.

Ferret out implications from the written discussion that provide insight and new direction for the issue or problem under investigation.

Bring out those aspects of the study that merit further study.

Give examples of learning experiences and fusion of horizons on the part of participants that took place during the research process. Relate the study to yourself in terms of what you learned and what role the study played in your life. Ricoeur's concept of enlarged self can be exemplified with illustrations from the researcher's own experiences. (See Appendix B for an example of analysis that depicts participant and researcher learning and fusion of horizons.)

Additional Data

Data collected from sources other than conversations may include reports or policy statements on organizations or communities related to the study; pertinent in-house or in-country journals or documents; correspondence, cleared by the sender; or other materials related to the subject at hand. Again, it should be noted that the researcher's own log derived from observation data and personal reflections is an important source of data and can enhance the text derived from conversations and the analysis.

The above process is a basic outline discussion. The discussion below provides additional detail, theoretical grounding, and examples drawn from participatory inquiry in a critical hermeneutic tradition.

Focus of Research Project

Habermas writes of an intimate relationship between knowledge and human interests. This relationship is based on an acknowledgment that subjects play an active and dynamic role in constituting the world they know and live in. Habermas's (1971) primary attempt in *Knowledge and Human Interests* is to radicalize epistemology by portraying the roots of knowledge in life rather than in a methodological science. The question remains as to whether Habermas has succeeded in establishing that there are precisely three cognitive interests (that is, technical, historical, and emancipatory), grounded in the natural history of the human species, which serve as the specific viewpoints from which our reality is apprehended. However, there appears to be from his argument, as well as other hermeneutic writers, substantial force (reason) to consider our interests as a point of departure for choosing a research issue and for interpreting what it means. There seems to be reason to follow our interests not only because of a personal proclivity toward an issue but also because the structure of the world to which we belong is shaped by our interests and our history, which, in turn, are the basis of the interpretation of our texts. Interests as part of our generative knowledge base are distinguished from an ideology of self-interest and minimal commitment to others — an ideology that has invaded Western society in the name of individualism. Our interests are starting points subject to change, for learning to see and understand differently, thus engendering new interests and practices. We could say that our interests are a present horizon.

The research position discussed in this book is essentially different from the positivist position, suggesting that we need to bracket out our interests in authentic research methodology lest we color or taint the data. Realistically, we do not exclude history or set aside our interests when we carry out research, but rather include history and interests as the basis for a fusion of horizons, interpretation, and new ideas. In his critical analysis of the Anglo-Saxon and continental schools of metascience, Radnitzky (1973: 224) points out succinctly, "There is no neutral standpoint outside of history upon which the cultural scientist could base himself." Our interests over time shape and to a certain extent constitute our history. Our interpretations cannot escape either our past or our present interests. Interests are similar to the prejudgments that are the conditions of our understandings. In addition to comprising in part the structure of our social life, interests need to be brought into the open before they can help us to remember and renew the authority and tradition that make up the context of our lives. This stance is far from the hermeneutic stance of Dilthey who thought that as cultural scientists we were restricted to merely a descriptive function. The social science research that often falls under the rubric of qualitative research frequently is grounded in the hermeneutics of Dilthey's claim that the process of interpreting a person or a text has no necessary effect on the self-understanding and practice of the researcher. Here, in the present writing, the claim is that research is not only a linguistic phenomenon, but a historical, social, and political activity as well, with our own interests as the starting point for inquiry. Only by traveling with our interests to the point of questioning what implications our interests have for our lives in community will we be able to place ourselves in a position of critic and see the contradictions in our lives.

The most critical reason for our interests to be the starting point of our research is that they provide an integrative medium for our search for knowledge and understanding. Often the more we understand something, the less we can accept another's meaning system for our own lives. For example, when enough of the people of Thailand collectively see the importance of their own history and their present position in the world economic and political context, the more likely they will be to adopt a critical and interpretive perspective of social development. Currently, it appears that this country predominantly accepts Western values and technology in the name of progress and development.

Our interests and the interests of others give meaning to our search and inquiry collaboratively over time. However, our interests, and their concomitant prejudices, need to be placed at risk in tandem with our everyday actions so that we may check their viability and appropriateness. In addition, interests provide a basis for learning, for learning takes place only in a context that has meaning for us. The nature of our knowledge and understanding is in a state of constant flux (what Maturana and Varela call "autopoesis"), and the research process as a whole for a group of participants can self-generate new interests and new understandings. A transforming and unfolding of interests is an important aspect of lifelong learning. Maturana and Varela (1980: 45) characterize an autopoietic system as a learning system. When we actively become aware of how and what we learn, we are in a better position to focus our lives and to create our own meaning systems to evaluate and direct our choices.

Background of Researcher

An important section of the research proposal and final project is one devoted to the researcher's professional background in addition to basic beliefs and interests that relate to the topic under investigation. To include this section enlarges the context in which data are read or interpreted. In hermeneutic research based on commitment and on conversations, a major goal is for both researcher and participants to change ideas and understandings about themselves and about the issues at hand. Any changes and new understandings recorded by the researcher enrich the text as a whole and give depth to the research project. The researcher's log or journal is integrated into the text that gives birth to the matter of the text, which in turn unfolds new worlds and new modes of being for the researcher and other readers.

Research Categories

The traditional review of literature for a research project purports to set the context for what has been written about the research interest at hand. This literature search is important for several reasons, including the idea that to unknowingly repeat what has already been carried out is not only a waste of time but also shows a lack of scholarship on the part of the researcher. A good review of literature will point to the areas in need of further inquiry. An additional reason for the review of literature in hermeneutic participatory research is to help determine the basic categories the researcher uses to place direction and boundaries on the inquiry. Categories reflect both the interests of the researcher and what aspects of a general topic writers in the field have designated as important.

Heidegger (1962: 44–45) points out that in the study of man there are two basic ways by which man's nature can be addressed and discussed. One is to study the entities that are related to man's being and the other is to study those entities that are obviously descriptive of man. The entities related to this second mode of man's character Heidegger calls categories. An entity that is of a categorical mode can be investigated and discussed by asking "what" (as opposed to asking "who," which relates to man's being). A "what" question refers to those aspects of man's character that stand out, which are "present-at-hand in the broadest sense." Those things that are present-at-hand are in front of us, they are obvious.

However, those things that are ready-to-hand are not obvious (for example, the being of a person or, in an everyday example, the hammer used in pounding a nail). We pay more attention to the characteristics of a person than one's being. One's being is not obvious. The nail receives our attention in hammering, not the hammer, which is almost like an extension of our arm. The hammer in a sense is not obvious; we do not take notice of it. It is ready-to-hand. Conversely, present-at-hand are those tools, things, or subjects that stand out in front of us. With them, we encounter something apart from us. They require us to make a decision about something.

In formulating a research project, categories need to be determined. Drawing from the basic idea of category used by Heidegger and applying it more directly to field-based research, a category is an idea or concept that stands out in front of the researcher. As one goes through a review of literature, one needs to think about developing certain categories that will help serve as parameters for the research project. Otherwise, the research project can be overwhelming in terms of size, or it can appear without direction.

In a review of literature one sees highlights or themes that can be noted in the questions writers ask within a tradition or discipline or in specific issues that shape an academic field. They can be the beginning of a research category. The researcher has the responsibility to make a decision about which categories will shape the research project. This is an important decision because categories play a dynamic role in the research. They carry the project forward, serve as markers for inquiry, provide the circumference of conversations, and serve as points or themes for discussion in analysis. They need to be well thought through; otherwise, they detract from the primary issue at hand.

The interests that a researcher carries to the review of literature often serve as initial category development. They cause the researcher to seek out certain aspects of the literature that may provide a focus and become one of the categories of the research project. For example, in the history and philosophy of science, a major question that has been of interest over some time has been, How do scientific paradigms change? Alternatively, to state it in a Collingwoodian manner, "On what occasions and through what processes do paradigms shift?" From this general question, a researcher may draw some guidelines for delineating a particular study or for shaping it in a particular direction. Rarely are categories discrete; rather they overlap and can even change during the research process if the researcher sees that the conversations in the field direct one to a theme or subject different from the original one(s). It is also possible to change the categories during the review of literature if interests shift or if the literature deems such a choice appropriate.

Within each category, the researcher attempts to ask questions that will promote a conversation about the topic at hand. These questions need not be asked in the exact same manner to each of the participants. In fact, it is rare that this happens because each participant brings a different history to the research conversation and soon after the first question is asked the conversation may take a slightly different route than it did in previous conversations. The researcher is in a position to make judgments about how far out of the way a conversation should go and when it should be drawn closer to the subject at hand. To do this and to have a natural conversation at the same time is not an easy task. It takes practice. Practice sessions are important, especially for beginning researchers. Categories help keep the research project in tow, but should not limit inquiry to predetermined designations. Important issues related to the subject under investigation may come up repeatedly in conversations and become a new category in the research project.

Celeste Gonzales (1991), in her research on educational policy-making on the national level in the Philippines, found that she had to change categories due to the kinds of conversations she encountered in her pilot study and at the beginning of her research project. Her explanation below is adapted from her dissertation work (1991: 75–81).

Research Category Change
Celeste Gonzales

I found I had to modify my categories from the original ones I established in my research proposal. My original categories and questions were as follows:

Category I: Moral/Ethical Know-how (Phronesis)
  What do you think education should be?
  How can current curricular policies be utilized, adapted or revised to accommodate moral issues?
  What are the political and social implications of a curriculum which advocates a core of ethics/moral knowledge?

Category II: Practical Application (Praxis)
  What does curriculum mean to you?
  How do you think teaching and learning should take place in schools?

What kind of curriculum policies are required to develop an educational system for the Philippines so that the paradigm development is consistent with our country's needs?

Category III: National Identity
Who is the Filipino? How would you describe him?
How shall education help mold the Filipino identity?
How do current curricular policies and practice reflect our history and tradition?

The modification was brought about by two factors. I carried out two pilot studies of my categories and questions, one in the United States and one in Manila. In Manila I discussed the categories and guide question with a college professor, a grade school teacher, and a curriculum specialist. They said that some of my questions I designed might not move the conversation to the topics I was interested in. For example, they pointed out that the participants might answer me with the Values Education Program in discussing questions 2 and 3 of the Phronesis Category. They explained that this program is promoted by the Department of Education, Culture, and Sports. However, I still asked my first three research participants the questions. Just as my pilot participants indicated, they answered me with the Values Education Program which is not the focus of my study.

Questions 2 and 3 were originally designed to create a conversation around the issues of phronesis which is ethics. However, I am interpreting phronesis slightly differently from the teaching of values. I am using the concept of phronesis as a form of ethical and theoretical knowledge and a moral integrated act that has to be part of effective policy-making.

It was at this point that I was convinced that there was a need for me to redefine my questions and to consider the suggestions of the three pilot participants because I was in a conversation that did not relate to what I thought would come from my original questions. I also realized that I needed to ask the participants about their thoughts and reflections on the state of Philippine education today in order to initiate our interview conversations. In adding questions and rephrasing/modifying some of the original ones, the participants started to engage in conversations that were more along the lines of what I was interested in. Once I engaged my participants to talk about questions which were clearer, they shared interesting insights and speculations on education and curriculum issues.

Tied in with the change in questions was the need to modify the original categories. As indicated above, my original categories were (1) Phronesis (ethical know-how); (2) Praxis (practical application); and (3) National Identity. No categories were removed. I added one category and combined Phronesis and Praxis under one category. I now have for the first category the state of Philippine education because my questions focused on the participants' assessment of Philippine education and their thoughts on education. This category provided the basis for the conversations on the next two categories. The second category focused on the role national identity plays in creating a curriculum that is more Filipino in orientation. I decided to put phronesis and praxis together because both are required for undergirding in curriculum policy-making and development. Phronesis is a stance that policy-makers have to take and acknowledge in order to carry out decisions that will lead to a more informed and relevant praxis in education. The modified categories, guide questions, and rationale for each category is presented below.

The categories served as the guidelines for the data collection and provided the structure for the conversation, reflection, and analysis. The guide questions provided the framework to initiate the conversations.

Category I: Philippine Education at Present

This category presents the current situation in Philippine education, what it means to people, what it has accomplished, what it fails to accomplish, how it has helped in national reconstruction, and how it might be improved to provide a more relevant and meaningful education to the Filipinos.

Guide Questions:
What is the Philippines going through right now?
How do you assess the present education system? What are your views, thoughts, reflections on it?
What is education for the Filipino?
What do you think education should be?

Category II: National Identity

Philippine education has passed through various stages of development. It also has been apparent that colonial influences permeate the curriculum. Education can create the context in which Filipinos could acknowledge where they are, orient themselves to reach understandings, and construct a Filipino identity. This involves bringing forth a collective identity that individuals and society establish together in an intersubjective relationship (Habermas 1979: 106–111). The core of this education, therefore, needs to be a Filipino identity since without this identity there's no prior departure for competition or cooperation among Filipinos and the world.

Guide Questions:
Who is the Filipino? How would you describe a Filipino?
How shall education help mold the Filipino identity?
How do current curricular policies and practices reflect our history and tradition?

Category III: Phronesis/Praxis in Policy-Making
Implications for Educational Curriculum

Phronesis (ethical know-how) defines what basic norms are needed in society. This involves judgment and moral knowledge which "allow man to determine what the concrete situation asks of him or to put it another way, the person acting must view the concrete situation in light of what is asked of him in general" (Gadamer 1988: 279). Bernstein (1983: 157) articulates the need for ethical know-how because "we are in a state of great confusion and uncertainly (some might even say chaos) about what norms or 'universals' ought to govern our practical lives." Phronesis is a form of reasoning or knowledge that calls for a prudent understanding of the situation and of other human beings. As Gadamer (1988: 288) says, "The person then with understanding does not know and judge as one who stands apart and unaffected, but rather, as one united by a specific bond with the other, he thinks with the other and undergoes the situation with him."

The nature of praxis (practical action) which is rooted in ethical know-how, is human activity manifested in speech and action. Praxis calls for reflection and understanding of situations in order for meaningful applications to take place. Bernstein (1983: 160) points out "that praxis requires choice, deliberation, and decision about what is to be done in concrete situations. Informed action requires us to try to understand and explain the salient characteristics of the situation we confront." It is from these constitutive elements that a relevant curriculum can come to be. Grundy (1987: 115) further elaborates that the principle of praxis would suggest that the curriculum itself develops through the dynamic interaction of action and reflection and the construction of the curriculum cannot be divorced from the act of implementation.

Phronesis and praxis provide the approach in placing curriculum policy-making within the social, political, and cultural contexts that interact with and help shape Philippine education.

Guide Questions:
What does curriculum mean to you?
What kind of curriculum policies are required to develop an educational system for the Philippines so that the paradigm developed is consistent with our country's needs?
What process should we follow when we engage in curriculum policy-making?

In retrospect, these categories served well my efforts to generate conversations that focused not only on a topic I chose for my dissertation, but more importantly, on a long time personal and professional interest that directs and shapes my life.

Research Questions

It is not an easy task to formulate questions that engage participants and researcher in an open and honest conversation, moving beyond winning or losing an argument, light banter, or professional jargon. Asking the right question is of critical importance in providing a context for knowledge and understanding — for preserving an "orientation toward openness" (Gadamer 1988: 330), in other words, for learning. Gadamer (1988: 328) describes the art of questioning:

The art of questioning is not the art of avoiding the pressure of opinion; it already presupposes this freedom. It is not an art in the sense that the Greeks speak of techne, not a craft that can be taught and by means of which we would master the knowledge of truth. . . . The art of dialectic is not the art of being able to win every argument. On the contrary, it is possible that someone who is practicing the art of dialectic, i.e. the art of questioning and of seeking truth, comes off worse in the argument in the eyes of those listening to it. Dialectic, as the art of asking questions, proves itself only because the person who knows how to ask questions is able to persist in his questioning, which involves being able to preserve his orientation towards openness. The art of questioning is that of being able to go on asking questions, i.e. the art of thinking. It is called "dialectic," for it is the art of conducting a real conversation.

There is a close relationship between asking a question and understanding. Gadamer suggests that it is this relationship that gives the hermeneutic experience its true dimension. Questioning is not the positing of, but rather the testing of, possibilities. Questioning is like the opening up of meaning, not merely recreating someone else's meaning. Asking a question opens up possibilities of meaning and, importantly, what is meaningful then becomes part of one's own thinking on the issue. Questions we do not ask are understood in a strange fashion — such as we know they are out of date, or we know they are meaningless. We have to understand before we can question. In other words, we understand that there is no question at hand. Gadamer (1988: 338) writes of the relation between understanding and questions: "To understand a question means to ask it. To understand an opinion is to understand it as the answer to a question."

Questions reflect the intensity of our ability to derive meaning from our past and the past of others. When we pose a genuine question about a text, and therefore a tradition, we go beyond mere reconstruction of what led to the question. Understanding tradition requires that the reconstructed question becomes part of our own comprehension of the past. In doing this we regain the concepts of a past that include our own comprehension of such ideas. Gadamer (1988: 273) calls this "the fusion of horizons." Specifically, Gadamer (1988: 337) writes, "that we understand only when we understand the question to which something is the answer, and it is true that what is understood in this way does not remain detached in its meaning from our own meaning. Rather, the reconstruction of the question as an answer, from which the meaning of the text is to be understood as an answer, passes into our own understanding." To ask a question about a text or a review of literature calls forth a particular relationship between the person posing the question and the text. A text does not speak to us in the same way as does another person, yet the back-and-forth of question and answer, whether it is between a person and a text or between two people, makes understanding appear as a reciprocal relationship. In this reciprocal relationship there is the anticipation of an answer expected. This anticipation presumes that the person asking the question is part of the tradition under consideration and is addressed by the tradition. Gadamer (1988: 340) explains that "This is the truth of the effective-historical consciousness . . . [in which we are] open to the experience of history . . . described . . . as the fusion of horizons of understanding, which is what mediates between the text and its interpreter." The fusion of horizons is the aim of hermeneutic research, which opens possibilities for our new understandings with concomitant actions.

Field-testing Conversation Questions

Field-testing or piloting one's questions, or guidelines for conversation, provides an opportunity to determine whether the questions or guidelines make sense. Piloting also provides an opportunity to practice carrying on a conversation rather than merely a question-and-answer interview. It also provides an opportunity to use the tape recorder to record the conversations. A malfunctioning tape recorder has on more than one occasion been the source of consternation.

Participants involved in the field testing of the questions may or may not be included in the general research project. If conversations held during the pilot provide a text that allows new understandings to emerge, these data can become part of the data collection and analysis part of the work. Until one has experienced trying to carry on a research conversation, Gadamer's writing on conversation is academic. After a few attempts, one can read Gadamer with a new understanding of what a conversation entails.

Participant Selection

Whether the research project is about educational and economic development in a third world country, teacher education in California, or international management programs, the researcher has the responsibility to be as prepared as possible before selecting people to participate. Participants can be nominated by professionals in the field. Alternatively, researchers can select and ask people they know personally. Additionally, the researcher can call people in the area of the research subject, explain the project, and ask for their participation.

Carolyn Nelson (1992) recollects her doctoral research on science education, her participant selection, her research questions, and the initial fieldwork attempt at carrying on conversations.

Participant Selection, Question Formation, and Research Conversations
Carolyn Nelson

Context:

The context of my research relates to my involvement in science education for the past 15 years. Four of those years have been spent in teacher education as an instructor of science methods classes and as a supervisor of student teachers. As a university instructor, I have observed that the majority of students who enter my science methods classes come with a distorted view of science; their orientation toward the subject is often negative and most, despite years of schooling, have limited knowledge about the nature of science or the information gleaned through scientific processes. In an effort to ferret out the reasons behind this appalling lack of exposure to scientific ways of thinking and working, I conducted a pilot study to query individuals involved indirectly and peripherally in the multiple facets of science education.

My participants included the following: a scientist/professor, a high school physical science teacher, and a high school science student teacher. My rationale for choosing these people is as follows.

A Scientist/Professor. As a member of the scientific community, the scientist holds the power to legitimate what question may be asked and what techniques may be used to seek solutions. He produces science knowledge and reproduces it in his students. In a sense, the scientist functions as the gatekeeper of all scientific knowledge. The product of his work is information that is added to the body of knowledge from his predecessors for verification through reproduction and for serving as a guide for future experiments. This information is then dispensed to the rest of society who cannot experience directly what the scientist experiences in his laboratory.

A High School Science Teacher. Millar (1989: 1) states that although scientists have produced detailed studies in the research laboratory, there have been very few comparable studies of the science teaching laboratory — i.e. the science classroom. The high school science classroom is, according to Millar, the "locus of those processes by which the scientific community replicates itself, and by which public understanding (or misunderstanding) of science is promoted." It is at this level that students should receive the most extensive "realistic" science of the K-12 education.

High School Science Student Teacher. The high school science student teacher's conversation should reveal the language of her institutional "training" and in doing so, unveil the ideologies and methods by which teacher educators replicated themselves.

The larger purpose of my work is to develop a conceptual framework for science education that reflects the communicative and historical nature of the new paradigm in science. This emerging paradigm is now challenging the dominant paradigm of Newtonian science. Applying T.S. Kuhn's (1970) description of how science knowledge is gained, accepted, and assimilated, it would seem that we are experiencing a crisis in science through which new paradigms emerge. As demonstrated in Maturana and Varela's *Autopoesis and Cognition* (1980), Prigogine and Stenger's *Order Out of Chaos* (1984), and David Bohm's *Wholeness and the Implicate Order* (1980), anomalies have crept into the dominant paradigm. The Newtonian view of science as a temporal, ahistorical, linear, mechanical system which can be knowable only by an objective observer no longer fits our current knowledge of science. The emerging scientific paradigm can be characterized as nonlinear, disorderly, unstable, diverse and temporal (Prigogine and Stenger 1984: xiv).

This paradigm shift provides an optimal time to consider alternative ways for teaching science that incorporate our communicative and reflective nature into the methodology. These alternative ways, while expanding the boundaries of science education, will provide us with other modes of interpreting and understanding science, thereby enriching and authenticating it. The Newtonian view of science promotes feelings of disconnectedness, irrelevancy, and inauthenticity. This narrow view of science is represented in textbooks as a collection of facts, theories, and methods. These texts become the received view for educating students in the ways of science. Kuhn (1970: 1) suggests that this view has come primarily from the study of finished scientific achievement and that "a concept of science drawn from them is no more likely to fit the enterprise that produced them than an image of national culture drawn from a tourist brochure or a language text." I believe this feeling of disconnectedness is prevalent because we do not understand how history, language, and ideology have influenced our understanding of science. However, because of our innate ability to communicate and to reflect on our historicism the possibility exists for a new orientation toward science; one that will reflect our primordial ways of Being in the world. My hope is that this new orientation will help students develop an authentic and meaningful view of science while creating a context for them, in Ricoeur's (1982: 182) words to "receive an enlarged self from the apprehension of a proposed world. . . ."

The disconnected view of science perhaps helps to explain why many people do not pursue science in higher education, why teachers do not enjoy teaching it, and why the general public often view scientists as the enemies of nature.

A new conceptual framework for science is significant because without an appropriate science curriculum, our students are mired in an antiquated and inaccurate account of themselves and their world. The new framework will create a context for students to have a more authentic view of themselves and their relationship to other individuals and the natural world, Moreover, this hermeneutical based framework holds significance for teachers in general, because we need to have an historical perspective for whatever we teach we well as learn. This perspective helps us understand the paradigm in which we live and the major paradigm shifts that have occurred heretofore. It also provides a depth of understanding that will enable us to experience what thinking, learning, and understanding really mean.

Research Questions and Rationale:

I designed my questions based on readings from critical hermeneutics and history of science. The following are two of the questions I asked my participants. After each question is a short synopsis of my readings that relates to the question and that grounded it for me.

1.   Tell me 3 or 4 of the most important scientific discoveries that have influenced biology. Tell me 3 of the most important scientific events of your personal /professional life.

Ricoeur (in Kearney 1984: 16–18) points to

the necessity to move from a pure phenomenology of reflective consciousness to a hermeneutic phenomenology which recognizes that the subject's retrieval of itself and of meaning requires a "detour" though the objective structures of culture, religion, society, and language. He defines hermeneutics as "the art of deciphering indirect meanings." Only by recognizing the various obstacles and opacities which the project of self-understanding encounters, and by thus resisting the facile solution of some "absolute synthesis" of knowledge which would contrive to resolve prematurely the conflict of interpretations, can we achieve an authentic grasp of the role of human creativity and imagination in spite of all the odds. . . . By retelling our histories, . . . a new set of events and facts are deemed to be relevant and claim our attention.

Ricoeur says it is impossible to experience pure self-reflection, that is, to remove one's self completely from one's prejudices. Gadamer (1976: 9) explains that it is "our prejudices that constitute our being. . . . They are simply conditions whereby we experience something." Self-understanding begins when we examine the objective structures of culture, religion, society, and language that constitute our prejudices. This is accomplished by retelling our histories. Ricoeur (in Kearney 1984: 22) suggests that it is "by retelling and recounting what has been, that we acquire an identity." Our personal history is a narration, he continues, that "preserves the meaning that is behind us so that we can have meaning before us."

2.   On what occasion and through what processes does one change his understanding about science?

In *The Structure of Scientific Revolutions* Kuhn (1970) presents a developmental schema of science beginning with normal science practiced under the guidance of a paradigm. One key impetus to the progression of normal science is the occurrence of anomalies — facts that were unexpected on the basis of the prevailing paradigm. Ordinarily, anomalies are resolved by improving our understanding of the paradigm as it applies to the dilemma. Sometimes, however, anomalies accumulate and persist to the point that we start to question the veracity of the paradigm itself. Then we have a crisis, from which — in order to resolve the apparent incongruities — new paradigms are suggested.

An example of this process occurred during the early twentieth century. During this period, new and revolutionary ideas were introduced into physics that opened the way to a new philosophical view, differing from the classical Newtonian view. The contradictions and inconsistencies of the old theories forced scientists to ascribe new properties to the time-space continuum and to apply these new properties to all physical phenomena. Einstein (in Capra 1982: 77) writes, "All my attempts to adapt the theoretical foundation of physics to this [new type of] knowledge failed completely. It was as if the ground had been pulled out from under one, with no firm foundation to be seen anywhere, upon which one could have built." Einstein's theory (Relativity) subsequently changed the way scientists view time and space.

Interview vs. Conversation

Posing my questions in a pilot study gave me the opportunity to see whether or not my questions were the kind that promoted a hermeneutic conversation, or merely a question and answer interview. Based on the writings of Ricoeur, Gadamer, Kuhn, and Heidegger, I designed questions that I thought would promote a context for conversation. However, in retrospect, I actually conducted two interviews (scientist and high school teacher) and one discussion that approached a conversation (student teacher). It was not until I began my actual research project that I had a genuine conversation during which there was a sense of play that Gadamer talks about. My participant was a professor of science.

There are two reasons why I believe my first two sessions were interviews and not conversations. First, the technical interest was so ingrained in my educational background that it was still operating at a subconscious level. Therefore, I was collecting data in the Newtonian sense of the term. In so doing, I felt I needed to control my variables by sticking to the script. Otherwise, comparison of the results would be invalid. Secondly, my understanding of the theory upon which my questions were grounded was inadequate. I was still reappropriating my own view of science based on the writings of Prigogine, Kuhn, Bohm, and Maturana and Varela. As the conversations and the research progressed I was able to think and imagine differently, and together the participants and I created new stories about teaching science.

Although most researchers formulate questions to guide their conversations, Dave Ancel (1995: 52–53) explains that instead of designing questions for his study, "An Interpretive Approach to the Mediation of Culture and Technology in the Global Workplace," he prepared a brief introduction to hermeneutic research and sent this along with his statement of the problem to his conversation partners. He writes: "This process went well in the three conversations I conducted in the initial field study. The clearer I became about the direction of my research the richer the conversations; the last of the three yielded by far the most insight to me. I continued with this approach in collecting the research data." Below are his introduction to hermeneutic research and his impressions about the conversations:

This project will explore concepts of work using interpretive (hermeneutic) theory. A key notion of this theory is that language is not a tool. The metaphor of "language as a tool" implies that people are separate from language and can manipulate it. Interpretive theory holds that humans live in language and can not be separated from it. It is in language that understandings, meanings and a shared sense of reality are created. Therefore, our conversations will be used as data for an interpretive analysis. I will record the conversation and transcribe it. then, I will critically review the text for meanings and understandings that may be disclosed. I will return a copy of the transcript to you along with a brief analysis. If you have any thoughts or comments we can continue our conversation and incorporate any new thinking into the data. Following you will find a statement of the problem I am investigating.

Following this introductory letter, I included a copy of my statement of research and background of the research. Our conversation thus had an anchor in the particular interests and concerns I put forth to launch the study. The to and fro of the questions and dialogue in the conversations thus held a certain consistency throughout the investigation.

Most researchers want to have some questions guiding the conversations. However, that choice may depend on the researcher's ability as a conversationalist as well as the background and experience of the research participants.

Entree to Research Site

Today many people who would be potential partners for interesting and revealing conversations are extremely busy. It is not always easy to enter a research site whether it is in a school, a corporation, or another country. Time constraints of participants in addition to legal restrictions in other countries pose challenges that the researcher must take into consideration when planning the project. From the experience over years of hermeneutic field inquiry, I found that most people want to talk about the issue at hand. Most participants are seriously interested in having a conversation; they especially appreciate a good listener, one who hears what they say and speaks on the topic.

If the research is to be carried out in another country, one can write to set up appointments; however, it is rarely possible to know beforehand all the people who will be involved. In some cases, one does not know anyone before leaving for another country but goes anyway. Often, the researcher is introduced to other people with similar interests who might contribute to the study. In addition, in talking with participants here in the United States, the researcher can gain introductions to colleagues in other countries. Participant selection and entree experiences of a researcher most often depend on one's personality, experience, and the nature of the research focus. Many times the participants who end up in the study and the matter of entree go hand in hand.

Most often participants fall into two categories: somewhat formal and informal. With formal participants, appointments and introductions have been made or the researcher has intentionally chosen various participants. However, as we all know, some of the most interesting, rewarding, and revealing conversations are spontaneous. The men and women who drive taxis in China give a far different view of the success of the four principles of modernization than does the party-line person. Both kinds of participants are essential for texts that unfold new possibilities.

Entree into any organization, society, community, or country requires timing, planning, and flexibility. What follows is an excerpt Craig Zachlod (1990: 59–62, 64–65) adapted from his dissertation research project on the education of U.S. managers for overseas assignment in multinational corporations. This process of participant selection and entree is in dramatic contrast to Jo Williams's discussion (see Appendix A) of her entree into Nepal for her research on community, education, and economic changes in Nepal (Williams 1990). However, the common denominator of these two kinds of entree is the importance of establishing personal relationships, whether they are formal or informal.

Research Entree into Multinational Management Education
Craig Zachlod

A conversation with Lewis Griggs of Copeland Griggs Productions resulted in the acquisition of a list of corporations in California that had acquired the film series "Going International." A letter was sent to sixty organizations describing the study, including an abstract of the approved dissertation proposal. Follow-up telephone contacts were made and the first 40 confirmations of appointments were self-selected as participants in the study. Of those actually contacted by telephone only two of the companies were deemed inappropriate for participation. In the first company the small number of expatriate employees, two, made participation of questionable value, but a copy of the dissertation was requested and a meeting at some later date was discussed. The second company, I was told during the telephone contact, was having difficulty with expatriate personnel and therefore was eliminating the expatriate presence and replacing all U.S. expatriate employees with foreign nationals. They didn't have the time to participate and expressed some anger, taking exception to a statement in the proposal abstract, which stated that "solely replacing U.S. expatriates with foreign nationals might not be the solution."

One of the companies on the list included Raychem Corporation in Menlo Park, California. While discussing the research project with an acquaintance, I was given the name of Gordon Markley, who was the acquaintance's brother-in-law and who worked with Raychem Corporation. I called Gordon Markley, who told me he was a technical advisor and employee of Raychem Corporation who travels to China every four months for extended six-week advisory-residency trips. I spoke with him twice by telephone, and he provided feedback on the conversation questions to be field-tested. We discussed his work, the study, and our common experiences in The People's Republic of China. He is currently overseeing the installation of two "harness shops," one in Shenyang Aircraft Company, the other in Chengdu. In addition to suggesting I contact individuals in his company who might be interested in my study, he told me that he believed Raychem was a good company to work for, and that they were successful in their China program while many other Fortune 500 companies were not.

David Markley introduced me to Raychem. Through this initial contact and pilot conversation I was introduced to a modern international company that was dependent on a relatively large expatriate work force. Gordon told me that Raychem was a company that thrives on the importance of its people and open communication as a basis for international business success. On Gordon's advice, I called the company, introducing myself and telling them about my study. To my astonishment, I was connected directly to the President and Chief Operating Officer of Raychem, Mr. Bob Halperin. It was a shock when Mr. Halperin personally answered the phone and was prepared to discuss my international management study, then and there, and its applicability to Raychem. After a congenial, but directed conversation, Mr. Halperin told me that Raychem was as successful as it was because they were open to research on many levels, and he directed me to contact Mr. Bill Mitchell, Vice President and Director of the International Company. Once again, the reception I received communicated to me that this company bore little resemblance to the formally structured hierarchical bureaucratic Union Carbide Corporation I had worked for several years ago in New York City. It also differed evidently from my more recent corporate experience as a middle manager with Aramco in Saudi Arabia which fostered a "don't-rock-the-boat" with questions attitude. I asked myself where were all the buffers to protect these high ranking corporate offices from employees and outsiders?

Throughout my experience with Raychem especially, but also with other multinational companies participating in this study, a tangible attitude of increasing communicative openness seemed to be a functional part of the success associated with practices in multinational organizations. These managers were communicative, practical, engaging, and responsive, bearing little resemblance to middle managers of the past paradigm ideal. Bill Mitchell met with me twice and arranged for me to meet with other officers in the company domestically and overseas. My meetings with Mr. Steven Fairchild, Vice President of International Administration, and Ms. Priscilla Gilbert, Manager of Expatriate Support Services, provided further information about the company and additional people to interview.

Entree for overseas began with the end of a domestic conversation. When each conversation with the domestic participants was concluded I asked them for referrals oversess. I explained that the second part of the research project would be conducted in China, Hong Kong, Malaysia, Singapore, Thailand, and Japan and would take place when the domestic conversations were complete. Did they have subsidiary offices in those locations? Who was the counterpart manager? Would that person be "in-country" during August? Who else in that location would be a good person to talk with about the overseas assignment? Would they be willing to write or fax to set up an appointment on such and such a date? Will any of those people be attending meetings in the United States between now and my departure? Do you think they will have time to meet with me while in the U.S.?

Many domestic managers went beyond my expectations to provide contacts and assistance for continuation of the study. Once participants themselves, they recognized the legitimacy and potential of the study. Some contacted not only their overseas counterparts but also suggested additional participants within their domestic organizations. I intentionally avoided any requests for financial or physical support overseas but encouraged any suggestions for networking or extending the scope of the research. When participants were not forthcoming with suggested contacts or our meeting time limited pursuit of the topic, I would request a copy of the annual report, a telephone directory of personnel, copies of the in-house newsletter sent to expatriates, typically any additional public or in-house documents that would help me learn more about overseas operations and identify contacts in the overseas locations.

When I arrived in-country I would begin telephoning as soon as feasible. I tried to set up or confirm a total of two or three appointments a day. Any more than two scheduled appointments per day would be unrealistic in places like Bangkok, Thailand or Guangzhou, China. Occasionally I would accomplish three meetings a day but this could only be done when I had appointments with members of the same company or with offices in close proximity. I also used information from those annual reports following-up and contacting the listed manager of the overseas subsidiary. When I succeeded I explained the study, his company's domestic involvement, and I would set an appointment.

After each day of research conversations, I would retreat to my room to listen to tapes and highlight notes from our conversations while thoughts were still fresh. Usually jet lag and distorted sleep patterns provided enough odd time for planning and thinking through the follow-up action, next day plan, and note making. Conducting future research I intend to carry at least two tape recorders and will summarize highlight excerpts on various topical tapes for later specific analysis.

When I had an evening free I would go out on the town in search of additional appropriate participants. For example, in Hong Kong, one sultry evening, at Ned Kelly's Last Stand, a local watering hole for expatriates, I met American and British television journalists, posted in Hong Kong, who had recently returned from Beijing after filming the Tiananmen Square massacre. They provided not only insights behind the headlines, but stories of adventure and important background information about the state of the expatriate community in China. They explained why it was probably useless for me to go to Beijing at that time. Most American managers and their families had been evacuated and were just returning to Beijing. "Things are a mess up there," they told me, "and you'll have a lot of trouble getting around and finding a place to stay. It's impossible." On their account and because my research time was limited, I decided not to go to Beijing but instead decided to spend more time with participants in south China and Singapore. Conversations with these expats provided not only important information about the state of affairs in China but continuing discussion about our own life-world experiences as expatriates. The interaction with these men and other expatriates in Guangzhou, Singapore and on the flight between Hong Kong and Bangkok reminded me that the expatriate community was not just executive managers working for multinational companies but a rich fabric of individuals who really comprised the context of my study. My impromptu and recorded conversations with several women, wives of overseas managers, at the American Club in Hong Kong; with a social service counselor and various administrative personnel in Singapore; with a female shoe buyer; an Oklahoma corporate president; and husband-wife teaching/administrative team at the American School in Guangzhou, while not the core group of my study, all contributed richly to a broader understanding of the international expatriate life-world environment.

Managers participated willingly in the study once a meeting was arranged. They were open, sincere, interested and overall invaluable resources for my understanding and, seemingly, also for their companies. The research was approached as a collaborative venture intended to help us better understand the expatriate experience through our conversations. The research questions that ground our discussions involved the participants by establishing communicative mutuality; that is, a basic agreement that the issues of expatriate assignment were important and of mutual interest, that we shared a language and tradition of expatriation, that the researcher had no ulterior motive other than the research, and we informally established a goal that through our conversations we might help both researcher and participant reach some new understandings about multinational corporate and expatriate life. In each case, the purpose and process of the study was clearly explained as a participatory research project for a doctoral dissertation.

About twenty-five percent of my prearranged meetings did not occur because of conflicts in schedules, managers being called away to meetings or other uncontrollable factors. Despite my perseverance, sometimes it was just not possible, in the culturally different time frame, to arrange an appropriate meeting without uncomfortably pressuring the participant. When this situation occurred I requested a substitute or a referral in the next country I was to visit. Probably the most helpful attitudes to develop are those that reflect humility, perseverance, and flexibility.

Upon the completion of my study I have continued in international educational development and consulting. In reflecting on my research experience I recognize a change in my attitude about multinational corporations. My original understanding and areas of concern were related to reducing or preventing premature terminations in overseas assignment. Those ideas were based upon the premise that by providing the right recipe for educating managers, problems of overseas living could be eliminated. My belief was that by internationalizing curricula we could better prepare people for the international cross-cultural experience. Indeed, preparation and appropriate curricula are still significant issues, and ones that ought to be a concern of multinational organizations. However, I no longer assume that organizations are so simplistic, or that positivistic recipes as prescriptive solutions can be applied to all situations. Rather a continuing communicative, evolutionary, educational model ought to be developed. This model needs to be developed in the context of each corporate community based in communicative action, continuous interpretation and understandings that recognize the place of language and shared traditions in the development of organizations. An organizational community or culture that values the overseas experience and utilizes that experience pragmatically within the organization improves understanding of domestic and overseas counterparts to the continuing benefit of employees and the company in general.

Personal conversations with the people at Raychem as well as dozens of others, both formal and informal, became the issues of this participatory research project and provided me with new horizons in the understanding of communications and the very nature of language as a socially significant action. In looking back at my entree into both domestic and international settings, I not only met many professionals who shared my interests, but through the conversations with the participants, both researcher and participants were educated. Most exciting were the new worlds of management that were created and the new professional relationships which were established, thus opening the way for my participants and myself to collaborate on future projects.

Researcher and Participant Collaboration

An important element in field-based hermeneutic inquiry is the opportunity for research participants to take an active role in the research process. The researcher gives transcripts of the conversations back to participants so they can see the course of the discussion, change parts of their conversation that, upon reflection, they disagree with, and/or provide additional insights. In such a process new understandings can emerge. In addition, it is possible for both researcher and participants together to critique existing activities and assumptions that were portrayed in the transcripts. This process can help build a community of memory among various participants setting the ground for continuation of work after a research project is completed. With research in a participatory and collaborative mode, the demarcation blurs between the end of the research project and the beginning of participants continuing the work.

Although there is an emphasis in field-based hermeneutic inquiry toward equalizing the relationship between researcher and participant, the responsibility for all aspects of the project in the end belongs to the researcher.

Research Conversations

Understanding is the proper achievement of language. However, often we study the role of language in our interpretation of a text or our conversations with others using the wrong approach. Traditionally, we study language in order to understand the text or a conversation. Rather, we need to see ourselves related to a text or in a conversation and from such vantage points approach the mystery of language. Actually, Gadamer (1988: 341) goes so far as to say that we are conversation and it is from this point that we need to approach language. In so doing, we can see that the commonalty between the study of a text and a conversation is found in understanding. Specifically, "the understanding of a text and the understanding that occurs in conversation . . . are [both] concerned with an object that is placed before them." When a person speaks to another, there is the concern of reaching agreement about an object, such as, what vocational education is in today's setting or how new teachers are socialized. What is the emerging relationship between technology and leadership? A more personal question would be "What is my place in the world?" There is the same concern with an interpreter understanding the object of which a text speaks. In each case, the understanding of the object must take place in language, "not that the understanding is subsequently put into words, but in the way in which the understanding comes about — whether in the case of a text or a conversation with another person who presents us with the object — lies the coming-into-language of the thing itself" (Gadamer 1988: 341). A point or object that we understand from a text or in a conversation is not brought into existence because we first know about it and then speak it or write or read it; rather it is brought into being because in language there rests the possibility of its existence in the first place.

For every conversation there is a common language or there is the creation of a common language among interlocutors. Partners in a genuine conversation must work out a common language and in such a language there is something placed in the center that is the focal point on which they exchange ideas with one another, agree, and disagree. This is not to say that we change our logic, adjust to the situation, adapt to our conversation partner, or use any other external mechanism to engage in conversation. Rather, people in a successful conversation "come under the influence of the truth of the object and are thus bound together in a new community." Further, Gadamer (1988: 341) explains that "to reach an understanding with one's partner in a dialogue is not merely a matter of total self-expression and the successful assertion of one's own point of view, but a transformation into a communion, in which we do not remain what we were." Following this line of reasoning, the individualistic ethos dominant in Western society does not prepare us well for successful conversations. Most often we are too fearful of losing control in a conversation to actually lose ourselves in a conversation and, thereby, carry on a genuine conversation with another person. How do we know when we move beyond babble or professional jargon, platitudes, or the question and answer motif in a conversation with our research participants? We know when we fall into a conversation, rather than conduct a conversation, and leave the conversation with different understandings than when we entered it.

Gadamer likens a successful conversation to the concept of play drawn from the field of aesthetics. About the experience of art, he argues that play refers to neither the attitude or the state of mind of the artist nor to the subjective reflection of player or spectator. Rather, play refers to the mode of being of the work itself. In a work of art one does not question an object that stands over or against a subject. Connecting this idea to what play is really like, Gadamer (1988: 92) writes that:

The work of art has its true being in the fact that it becomes an experience changing the person experiencing it. The "subject" of the experience of art, that which remains and endures, is not the subjectivity of the person who experiences it, but the work itself. This is the point at which the mode of being of play becomes significant. For play has its own essence, independent of the consciousness of those who play. Play also exists — indeed, exists properly — when the thematic horizon is not limited by any being-for-itself of subjectivity, and where there are not subjects who are behaving "playfully." The players are not subjects of the play; instead play merely reaches presentations through the players.

Play reaches presentation through the players if the player is lost in the play and thus fulfills its purpose. In playing a game, it is the game that masters the player, not the reverse. This is a significant distance from the Cartesian perspective where the active subject masters the game. Truth or being or a game is an ontological event that is disclosed to us in the present. In the case of reading a text, "in its deciphering and interpretation a miracle takes place: the transformation of something strange and dead into a total simultaneity and familiarity. This is like nothing else that has come down to us from the past." When we read something that has been handed down to us, it is a testimony to and an achievement of "the sheer presence of the past" (Gadamer 1988: 145). For the truth or being or game to be disclosed to us, we must allow ourselves to stand in the world created by the game, the art, the conversation, or whatever form. Speaking about art, R. E. Palmer (1969: 168) writes, "when we see a great work of art and enter its world, we do not leave home so much as 'come home.' We say at once: truly it is so. The artist has said what *is*. . . . The understanding of art does not come through methodically cutting and dividing it as an object, or through separating form from content; it comes through openness to being, and to hearing the question put to us by the work."

Yet, as we enter this new world, we understand it only because we are already participating in the structures of self-understanding, which, in turn, make it truth for us. The artist, as does a researcher, creates a work — a truth that abides. The fusion of the truth or being that is represented with the form of the art is "so complete that something new comes into being." This something new is the result of a mediation of knowledge that is the "experience of beholding the work of art [which] makes this knowledge shared knowledge" (Palmer 1969: 169). What this means is that the work of art works *in* becoming experienced, it transforms the experience. The work of art has its authentic being in this fact.

The subjectivity of one who experiences is not what endures over time, rather it is the work itself. Palmer (1969: 174) writes that it is at this point that "the mode of being of a game becomes important." The authenticity of a game also resides in the fact that the game has its own nature independent of the consciousness of the players. The dialogical and ontological nature of art and a game serves as a model for Gadamer's hermeneutics and, in turn, for field-based research carried out in a hermeneutic tradition.

Every conversation requires that speakers speak the same language or that translators are present, which to some extent changes the process of understanding. When translators are involved there are two interpretations: the speaker's and the interpreter's. Translators need to involve themselves with the meaning to be understood in the conversation or it is not a translation; thus, translation is both interpretive and technical in nature. When carrying out research in a second language setting, the researcher who does not speak the second language should attempt to choose a translator who has some background and interest in the topic under consideration.

Simply said, Gadamer (1988: 347) states that, "A conversation is a process of two people understanding each other." Therefore, each person needs to be open to each other, truly accept the other's point of view as worthy of consideration, and understand what is said, as opposed to understanding the other person saying it. In this process the objective rightness or wrongness is the thing that has to be grasped laying the groundwork for agreement, or otherwise, on the subject. Important to note here is that in this process one does not relate to the opinion of the other but to one's own view. Here is where we risk our prejudices. Our own horizon with which we come to a conversation (either with another person or with a text) is the standpoint or starting point of the conversation — it is the meaning we carry to the conversation and that which ones brings into play. When we make our own that which is said in the conversation or in a text, our horizon has changed; the present (what is alien to us) has fused with the past (what is familiar to us).

What follows are reflections of Celeste Gonzales (1991: 66–69) on an excerpt of one of her conversations with one of her doctoral research participants in Manila. The general topic of conversations for her research was curriculum development for the Philippines through phronesis and praxis in policy-making. In this excerpt, the focus of the conversation is on text and its relationship to curriculum. It shows how the traditions of both the researcher and participant play a critical role in bringing forth new understanding — in this case on the part of the research participant.

A Conversation on Curriculum
Celeste Gonzales

Most of my conversations with the participants were dynamic. There were instances I did not have to ask the question I prepared as our conversations flowed naturally, touching upon the points I had in mind. I observed that as I was engaging in more conversations, I was sharing with my participants what the other participants had shared with me. These conversations gave my participants an opportunity to think, reflect, and verbalize their thoughts on educational issues. I felt that because they were given a chance to share and be active partners in the research project they were encouraged to generate new knowledge and reach new understandings. I was also able to share with them the potential of research conversations and the possibilities of hermeneutic participatory research.

Because of the spirit of involvement and partnership these conversations promoted, I experienced a more personal relationship with my participants. Mrs. Lala Castillo wanted to read more on critical hermeneutics so I lent her two of my books. Brother Andrew Gonzales gave me a book on the development of Asian universities. Dr. Wilfrido Villacorta asked me to sign his guest book and we exchanged addresses. Mrs. Estelita Capina and I have kept in touch since our conversations.

Upon further reflection, I realize that these conversations brought forth a stronger shared meaning of our everyday life. Part of the reason for this was the typed verbatim transcriptions completed while I was still in Manila sent to the participants for their reflection and critique. In presenting these full and unedited transcriptions of our conversations to the participants, the participants could validate their own contribution to the research project. Further, they could see how we in conversation are more than we are in isolation and how ideas and new understandings come forth.

Follow-up conversations with participants were carried out to discuss with them any changes in the transcripts, to fill in gaps in the first conversations, to clarify issues, and to put the issues and information in context. As Keiffer (1981: 36) writes, when transcriptions are given back to the participants, they are able "to speak more intimately and effectively to all the issues raised." This process also enabled the participants and me to reflect more deeply upon our assumptions, reach an understanding on the history of the problem, look into possibilities for the future and create alternatives for a more powerful and practical curriculum for the Philippines.

As an example, one of my participants, B. Santos, and I discussed how the rise of the Propaganda Movement during the Spanish period brought about the availability of printed books (texts) to the Filipino people. According to her, "texts raise our consciousness. The distribution of texts breaks down boundaries." She went on to say that a text is something we can invoke which enables us to read and rethink again in another context. She further added: "It is never erased for as long as it is not destroyed. It becomes a repository of consciousness and ideas." Though she basically is talking about printed books, I realized she had some basic understanding of what a text is. I then ventured into sharing with her how my vision of a text has expanded and how it can open us to possibilities. I also added how my whole research process can be looked at as a text and how curriculum can be a text. The following is an excerpt of our conversation and how new meaning about curriculum was brought forth.

CG. When I transcribe my interviews, they will also be texts. And when we do interpretations or an analysis of it, it opens us to other possibilities.

BS. Exactly.

CG. We are not saying that the traditional scientific or the analytical way is wrong. Both the traditional way and the field-based hermeneutic way are empirical — we collect data. But we often have a way of thinking that if it is empirical it involves numbers. I am doing my research this way because it is in our conversation and our language that we reveal ourselves — what we are and who we are.

BS. That's right. It is our chance to encounter and to participate.

CG. I also want to look at curriculum as a text.

BS. Exactly.

CG. And not just as a listing of subjects or courses. There is interaction with a text. When you read a text, it changes you. Your horizon changes.

BS. Yes.

CG. When you read that very same text at another time, something has already happened from the time you last read it to the time you are reading it again.

BS. That's right.

CG. A history is there. A memory has been created. In the text are our memories.

BS. That's right.

CG. When you read it again, you again come to a new understanding and of course you would have already reflected on what you have read.

BS. That's right. I understand what you are saying. If you tell me to read the curriculum as text I will say that the curriculum has a narrative.

CG. Yes.

BS. And it takes the narrative of a little child if it's the primary school. As a narrative it dramatizes or depicts specific climaxes or points of high interest. Educators should have identified these points in the life of the young boy or girl and emphasized these points. They should have organized the narrative into pockets of texts proper for that portion or phase of the child's life.

CG. Yes. Everything that we are is a story. There's a story in our lives.

SB. That's right.

CG. It will always have a political and social implication.

SB. That's right. So we say then that in our narrative of Philippine education is woven the narrative of colonization in the Philippines.

CG. Right.

SB. If you study the curricula of the different schools here and sort out the narrative. . .

CG. Then we get a story of who we are, get to know ourselves, and what our culture and our tradition is.

SB. Exactly! Exactly!

The limit of SB's horizon of curriculum was changed to include a different, or alien, understanding of curriculum, one that encompasses the life story of a child and of a people with a political and social meaning which creates a basis for memory to be grounded. It is in such a memory that we, as Filipinos, as well as other peoples, can act — namely to reflect, critique, and renew our lives. This concerted act is not technical in nature, but calls for an ethical stance, for wisdom on the part of people in charge of designing curriculum policy. The ethical dimension of policy-making is especially important in times of political and social upheaval which the Filipinos are now experiencing. Coming to new understandings is a fusion of one's horizon with a foreign idea, in this case, the use of narrative and story for educators.

This excerpt illustrates that through our speaking we risk our previous understandings and prejudices. In such an act of risking we can come to new understandings. As previously described (Herda 1990: 52), "The language we speak is essentially open to understanding different cultures or alien horizons. It is through the fusion of horizons, which are finite but not limited, that we risk and test our prejudices." It is in the risk that we have the opportunity to learn. However, without an orientation to reaching an understanding with another, we have only strategy in dialogue rather than communication in conversation. Celeste and Benildo had a conversation.

Although not all conversational encounters in field-based hermeneutic research result in a fusion of horizon on the part of either of the speakers, true conversation is the goal of the researcher. Such conversation provides the opportunity for learning.

Creation and Analysis of Text

The text enables us to communicate with each other as researchers in a profession, as researchers in concert with participants, and as readers of the text over time. The text does not belong to the researcher or the participants. However, it is the text that connects us and gives us a way to communicate.

There is more than one text created in field-based hermeneutic research. One text is created when the conversations are transcribed. In this process the discourse is fixed in writing, and the speakers are separated from what they said. This is part of the distanciation process. The meaning of what is said surpasses the event of saying.

Another text is created when the researcher selectively presents from the transcription texts a story about the issue at hand, drawing quotes to ground the narrative. The data that make up the second text include the reading and reaction of the participants to the transcribed text. This presentation is a text that tells a story. However, this act is not comprised of simply adding one episode to another. The object is to configure a totality out of scattered events.

In traditional qualitative research methods, one type of analysis a researcher can do is content analysis. In this process the object is to structure meaning out of the content by applying a systematic process of coding. However, in telling a story about the transcriptions and the experiences of data collection, the point is to discover a plot. Plot takes primacy over structure (Ricoeur 1982: 274–287).

A deeper plot is discovered in a third text utilizing the second text and the critical hermeneutic literature in which narration reveals an order that is more than the actual events and conversations in the research. Ricoeur (1984: 22) describes this process when he writes that, "There is always more order in what we narrate than what we have actually lived: and this narrative excess of order, coherence, and unity is a prime example of the creative power or narration." The act of narrating preserves the history that is behind us so we can have a future. The historical meaning — what took place during the research process as well as an account of the memories of the participants — is preserved in the text so that we can have meaning in front of us. The text opens up a world of possibilities. However, these possibilities only come out of a discipline of sorts — one that reflects the researcher giving order to conversation events and historical episodes by retelling and recounting what has been.

The researcher is repeating a story that includes parts of the lives of the participants and the researcher. In many cases the retelling of the story or history much more involves the participants than the researcher.

The researcher as narrator — the researcher is more of a narrator than an analyst — calls upon productive imagination in the invention and discovery of plots grounded in quotes from conversation and theory. In the narration there is the combination of context, circumstance, voice, and potential guidelines for future actions. In Appendix B, Abascal-Hildebrand's analysis of a conversation she had with a member of the Thai Economic Affairs Consulate concerning the economic development in Thailand shows how a conversation moves and the implications for play in a conversation. In addition, she shows how, through the conversation, a text is born that can provide new possibilities and ideas for development.

Appropriation of possibilities is made possible by a series of acts. As discussed above, the discourse about the matter at hand, the background of the problem, and the traditions carried with it are fixed in writing and become a text. This text captures the past and projects a future.

The productive imagination of the researcher is challenged to discern the plot that can provide the direction for future policies and actions. How we do this is, in part, the writing of the text, the presentation of the plot, additional conversations, and the living out of our lives — which, in turn, gives birth to new research projects. Ricoeur (1982: 185) translates the German term *Aneignung* (appropriation) to mean making one's own what was initially alien. Ricoeur further writes that "the aim of all hermeneutics is to struggle against cultural distance and historical alienation. Interpretation brings together, equalizes, renders contemporary and similar." Thus through interpretation of the analyzed text, we can find new relationships with strangers as well as with friends. The interpretation of the text is complete when the reading of it releases an event in our lives whereby we understand each other anew, and we learn how to address our social challenges in a different light, one that gives each of us a future with dignity.

RESEARCH IMPLICATIONS — LEARNING
AND COMMUNITY

If as Gadamer says, understanding is the proper achievement of language and, as Heidegger says, language is the house of being, then understanding has to do with who we are. Learning without understanding often is set apart by what we score on multiple choice answer sheets. The score often represents information we have gathered or remembered. Learning must go beyond the score to include understanding as well as a change in our present and our history — a fusion of horizons that happens when we make our own what was once alien. This action, however, does not take place in solitude. It is a social act in concert with another. As Herda and Messerschmitt (1991: 24) state: "Language involves learning when viewed as an interactive process among speakers rather than a grammatical utterance. Learning here is seen as the constant process of interacting, reflecting, and transforming one's thought processes, and even one's philosophy, in addition to one's ability to act in a responsible manner. Learning in this non-technical sense thus opens and sets different limits on the capacity to identify and solve problems and make decisions."

When we think of learning as a social activity, we move away from the idea that learning is the acquisition of knowledge of, or skill in, study, instruction, or experience. It goes beyond adding to one's store of facts or a change in behavior. For example, in organizations the question often asked is: "How do we solve such and such a problem?" In addition, trainers are brought in to teach problem-solving and decision-making techniques. The first thing to do, however, is to identify the actual problem. Problem-solving and decision-making processes have received attention in the literature on organization at the expense of teaching managers and administrators to think about the nature of the problem. This latter activity is far more philosophical than it is technical. It requires discussion and conversation with others to reach a conclusion grounded in action about what things mean and the way things are done. This activity involves changing people's patterns of thought and action, which, in turn, happens only when an individual has achieved a fusion of horizons.

If this line of reasoning continues, one shortly sees that the culture of individualism is a deterrent to at least some forms of learning — learning that entails understanding. We cannot understand unless we move from one horizon to another. Our horizons are finite, but they are not limited. It is in relationships that we come across new worlds, new ways of doing things. It is in relationships that we can have a backdrop with which to see who we are, to learn, and to change our history. An individual cannot do these things alone. Our society has for several decades celebrated individualism, but now many people are beginning to critique the price they paid for individualism and think about different kinds of relationships — ones birthed in community (Bellah et al. 1985).

When we think about relationships, often they are grounded in therapeutic or self-affirmation needs. However, a relationship that exists for helping the other or one that is grounded in a covenant rather than in a contract is a different kind. Businesses are now looking into the need to create a context in which relationships can develop that is intimate and inclusive. Indeed, some companies now recognize that a covenant among people is more important than a structural change in their attempt to meet today's business challenges (De Pree 1990).

In traditional social science research that follows a functionalist or positivist paradigm, assumptions that form the basis of ideas on learning focus on behavior, intervention, and structure — models of segmentation and fragmentation. Learning is believed to be individualistic in nature. However, research in the natural sciences (Prigogine 1980; Gould 1982; Watson 1980; Sheldrake 1982; Pribram 1974, 1976; Maturana & Varela 1980) supports the idea that our prejudices, interactions with others, history, reflection, and imagination all are important in learning and moving from one place in our knowledge and understanding base to another. Although accretion, building up information, is one kind of learning, it is not the critical element in a learning process. We learn by thinking differently and applying new understandings in our everyday lives. It is in application of what we learn that personal judgment, ethics, and responsibility come into play.

From the present discussion on hermeneutics, we note the central role of language in understanding. If we equate learning with understanding we have a different kind of learning than if we equate learning with acquiring knowledge that can be represented by scores on tests. Important as it is to have at hand the kind of knowledge that is often represented by scores, it is more important to teach learners how to reach understanding. This is the case because in understanding we do not take on someone else's meaning system (a passive learner), but rather work through our own along with others (an interactive learner).

Learning is more suited to a community model of, rather than a model based on, the individualism inherent in a functionalist or behaviorist model. The research model posited in the present text relies on community for it to work, and, at the same time, strengthens existing communities or helps to build new communities. However, the U.S. culture is characterized by an individualistic mode of living and learning, even though there are many programs or ideas that propose a collective philosophy, such as collaborative teaching, unity through the celebration of diversity, participatory decision-making, participatory leadership, and cooperative learning to name a few. Such philosophies or programs suggest that each of the partners involved meets the other at the halfway mark and that somehow collaboration or cooperation will take place. I think this is the general intellectual motif of these models. At times a suggestion is made that someone has gone more than half way to try to solve the problem. Built into such a statement is the expectation that they deserve something special for having done so. The general U.S. ethos does not support the idea that it is all right to give more than one receives. A true collective philosophy lived out in everyday lives requires that our idea of justice shifts from one where everything is divided equally, or where we receive equal and just rewards for whatever we do that is positive, to a philosophy whereby we allow ourselves to give more than we receive and in so doing build communities that are caring and supportive. It is in such communities that we can learn.

In field-based hermeneutic research, we see that the responsibility to learn is on each individual. Learning takes place because someone risks prejudices with the consequence of one's history including something new. Yet, it is not in an individualistic mode that such change takes place. Placing one's prejudices, or prejudgments, at risk happens against a backdrop. There needs to be another person's tradition, culture, or history that comes to the foreground in the presence of someone who, in turn, sees his own past and reflects on it. Two people in conversation, as discussed above, provide a setting in which such learning can take place. It does not automatically happen; it is an intentional, reflective, and imaginative act.

One should not think that somehow there is a better or different world because a person changes a little or that the histories of two people will merge to make a better one. We may glean ideas from others to make our own lives better. However, a personal act on our part is required to make our lives better or to work with others in a different mode. To change our lives and our understanding is more a responsibility than our right. When people demand their rights to gain a better life, they are relying on others to do it for them. The bottom line is that we do it ourselves or it is not done. This is not to say that we do not have an obligation to help others see new possibilities and to help create the context in which such changes take place. In the end, it is our responsibility to think differently, to learn, and to act differently. Field-based research in a hermeneutic tradition can help bring forth community motifs that engender conversation, reflection, and new bases for action.

Once we have found a new truth, spoken to us through our tradition of which we risked part, we cannot say that now we are alone in this discovery. We are not. Maturana and Varela (1980) tell us that we are constitutively social. If this is accurate, we need to attempt to come to community, not in the sense of a collection of individuals, but in an ontological sense — we are who we are from a community, not just similar individuals gathered together. When this happens we have, at best, what Bellah and colleagues (1985) refer to as life enclaves.

I do not suggest that in a research project the researcher and the participants necessarily will create a community, but the possibility for establishing a community in which people converse and understand each other is the anticipation of field-based hermeneutic research. This anticipation serves as a directive force for the research project. In other words, field research in a hermeneutic tradition implies a directional process rather than a one-, two-, three-step methodology.

Mere understanding, however, does not guarantee that we understand the truth of a situation. In the hermeneutic task, something happens to us — the interconnection of event and understanding. It is possible to understand this interconnection only if we sever ourselves from Descartes's position on the distinction between the subject and the object in knowing. Most social scientists view the world as the object of language. The researcher is the subject who through research can control objects studied. This view is further entrenched in their preparation for survey research where the data collected are thought to represent, in a neutral sense, the empirics in the world of education, business, nursing, or other applied fields. Each of these worlds is made into an object — more specifically, an object of language. The researcher is looking at the world under investigation as a disinterested outsider. This kind of objectivity demands that the researcher take the position of an onlooker. As Toulmin (1982: 254) warns, we "can no longer view the world as Descartes and Laplace would have us do, as rational onlookers, from outside. Our place is within the same world as we are studying, and whatever scientific understanding we achieve must be the kind of understanding that is available to participate within the processes of nature, i.e. from the outside."

Rationality in the received view of research is often thought of as a logical or linear thought process carried out by a researcher in a position external to the data. The goal is to collect data and put them in a form that represents and controls the world under investigation. The world of the researcher and the world one studies are separate from one another. However, in the histories of, and discussions among, scientists, we are beckoned to reexamine the process of science and the consequence of learning.

Rather than merely a researcher and data to be observed, counted, and controlled based on the subjective-objective distinction, there exists in real life science communities and human judgments. Our transformation into this community encounters a shift in our model of rationality from one that searches for determinate rules to one that emphasizes interpretation.

In debates and discussions among Thomas Kuhn, Karl Popper, and others (for example, Lakatos & Musgrave 1970), the implicit norms, ideals, and understanding were made visible. Although no overall agreement to date has been reached, a picture of science has emerged, which follows different images than the traditional rationalist and logical empiricist ideas of science. New words and images, such as community, interpretation, judgment, participation, and history, are important in understanding how scientific research actually takes place and how we choose one theory or datum over another. These readings on science do not easily penetrate our ideas of learning as demonstrated in our schools, especially the ways we test for achievement — and even more importantly what we think is important to evaluate. Most of our tests are designed to measure retention of information, not understanding. Maturana (1980: 45) writes that "Learning is not a process of accumulation of representation of the environment, it is a continuous process of transformation of behavior through continuous change in the capacity of the system to synthesize it. . . . It does not play the game of categories. And it does not interrelate disciplines, it transcends them."

Learning is a transformative process through experience that takes place over time. It is a historical and interpersonal process that overrides the subject-object dichotomy. Our challenge now is to change our ideas about the nature of science and, in so doing, our ideas about research and learning concomitantly will change. The student who can use the Newtonian paradigm for solving a particular problem and the interpretative paradigm for questioning another kind of problem stands in the wake of new understandings and new possibilities. This learning capacity is not technical and logical in nature. It is interpretive, imaginative, and judgmental. Making appropriate judgments is the critical key to learning. Moreover, we need to recognize that the judgments we make have moral implications. One does not learn about morality, however, by taking a class that teaches a subject called ethics. As Aristotle points out in his *Ethics*, moral principles cannot be the object of a course or body of knowledge that can be taught. Rather, we are always already in the position of having to act and must already possess and apply moral knowledge. Moral knowledge, as presented by Aristotle, is distinguished from technical knowledge and from the guiding principles of the unchangeable law of the heavens. Moral knowledge is concerned with right living, and the implications of our moral judgments need to be thought about and discussed throughout the teaching and learning of all disciplines.

Most often, it is difficult for people to change the groundwork from which they see the world. The ideology, lifeworld, or paradigm that governs our lives will not be visible to us without reflection and study of our assumptions and the language we use.

The psychologically constructed visual duck-rabbit paradox is used to illustrate the way in which our thinking, understanding, and seeing change when we use one paradigm as opposed to another. In Figure 3.1 the logical image is a duck, but one might also see the rabbit (from Hanson 1969: 95). This difference in thinking and perception is characterized more by creativity and imagination than by synthesis and analysis usually associated with high-level thinking abilities. Although the example of the duck-rabbit image does not make any significant statement about who one is or might become, it does help make the point that to see something different we move out of a tradition — in this case of seeing the duck (or rabbit).

Seeing something differently, whether it is a picture, a problem, or a question, requires a shift in us, and the intensity or significance of the shift has to do with the intensity or significance of the issue at hand. Changing

FIGURE 3.1

who we are in relation to others in a community or society involves changing forms of power and authority, which, in turn, involves a change foremost in oneself. What we risk in seeing a duck as opposed to a rabbit is obviously different than what we risk in assuming responsibility for our own freedom as opposed to believing someone else can give it to us through legislated rights, or what we risk in carrying out a survey as opposed to carrying out a conversation in the Gadamerian sense. The duck-rabbit example is not about a fusion of horizons, but it helps one see the nature of the learning enterprise.

When people begin to read hermeneutic literature, one of the greatest barriers to initial understanding is the everyday so-called common sense derived from Newtonian logic they carry with them into an attempt to learn something new. What passes as facts in our lives, in our science or social science, reflects the pictures we have of the world, our modes of expression, the character of our perceptions, our concept of time, and our understanding of tradition. We tend to reason that we learn when we change our behavior or memorize new data. Actual learning occurs when we change and fuse our horizons with something different and in the process become different. Learning is more an ontological activity than an epistemological activity. We do change, and consequently how we act can change. Risking our prejudgments is different than learning a new behavior. The act of learning does not happen in isolation; it only happens in a relationship with another, yet remains one's own responsibility.

The traditional relationship established between subject and object in science, with implications, for example, for learning in educational curriculum, is one where a subject, in an effort to objectively know the world, separates from the object. Grounded in this separation is the attempt to coordinate the subject and object through a concept of belonging that Gadamer (1988: 418) says we "won from the impasses of historicism." In the traditional research models in social science, there are two ways to establish this coordination. One way is to institute objectivity in a science project, such as in experimental or survey designs, and another way is to establish subjectivity as a viable alternative, for example, by somehow ethnographically grasping the truth from the research subjects — as in the pre-Heidegger kind of hermeneutics. In each case, whether the route is objectivity or subjectivity, attempts in establishing the facts or the truth are based in method. It is assumed that, in both cases, a structure exists in the world that we could know at times objectively (that is, through a survey) and at other times subjectively (that is, through an ethnography). In hermeneutic theory, one seeks to show not the relationship between subject and object, between the structure of the world and our knowledge of it, but rather the interconnection between event and understanding.

In arguing the hermeneutic case, Gadamer says the relationship between the subject and object must be thought about as the Greeks did. Gadamer (1988: 418) explains:

When it is a question of understanding the supra-subjective powers that dominate history, the Greeks have something over us, for we are entangled in the knots of subjectivism. They did not seek to base the objectivity of knowledge on subjectivity. Rather, their thinking always saw itself as an element of being itself. Parmenides considered this to be the most important signpost on the way to the truth of being. The dialectic, this expression of the logos [word], was not for the Greeks a movement performed by thought, but the movement of the object itself that thought experiences.

In metaphysics, the science grounded in objectivity, the concept of belonging between subject and object is seen as the relation of the mind to the structure of what exists. However, in hermeneutics the experience is not one of an interconnection of subject and object, but rather an interconnection of event and understanding — of tradition and its interpreter. There is an inward communion between tradition and its interpreter. The fundamental difference here between metaphysics and hermeneutics is that an event happens, it is an action, a process. The object, coordinated or interconnected with the subject, is an event that happens. From the perspective of the interpreter, Gadamer (1988: 419) writes that

"Event" means that he does not, as a knower, seek his object, "discovering" by methodological means what was meant and what the situation actually was, if slightly hindered and affected by his own prejudices. This is only an external aspect of the actual hermeneutical event. It motivates the essential methodological discipline one has towards oneself. But the actual event is made possible only because the word that has come down to us as tradition and to which we are to listen really encounters us and does so in such a way that it addresses us and is concerned with us.

The object in this event means a working out of itself as in genuine conversation and a new appropriation of tradition where something emerges that is contained in neither conversant alone.

Critical to an understanding of learning in this hermeneutic tradition is the primacy of the dialectic found in hearing. Hearing, as opposed to seeing, is the basis of the hermeneutic experience. You can look away, but you cannot "hear away" (Gadamer 1988: 420). The dialectic in hearing is found in the acknowledgments that one who hears is also addressed and that one who is addressed must hear, whether he wants to. Gadamer (1988: 420) notes that "whereas all the other senses have no immediate share in the universality of the linguistic experience of the world, but only offer the key to their own specific fields, hearing is a way to the whole because it is able to listen to the logos." Language opens a new dimension in learning, in contrast to all other experiences, "a profound dimension whence tradition comes down to those now living. . . . We belong to elements in tradition that reach us." We are not ever able to claim freedom because everyone "who is in a tradition — and this is true, as we know, even of the man who is released into a new apparent freedom by historical consciousness — must listen to what reaches him from it. The truth of tradition is like the present that lies immediately open to the senses" (Gadamer 1988: 420).

This is not an immediate sensibility but one that requires the hearer, who in interpreting a text, "relates its truth to his own linguistic attitude to the world." The event that takes place in all understanding is this linguistic communication between present and tradition. As Gadamer (1988: 421) points out, "language constitutes the hermeneutical event proper not as language, whether as grammar or as lexicon, but in the coming into language of that which has been said in the tradition: an event that is at once assimilation and interpretation." We understand when we see ourselves in the tradition in question. What reaches us from within the tradition we must listen to whether it is a spiritual or intellectual dynamic.

For example, intellectually, when begin to see research questions designed not so much to elicit an answer as to sustain a conversation we will see ourselves in a different tradition — a hermeneutic one rather than a positivist or analytic one. The event of conversation lends itself to understanding. The act of reading and coding responses on a survey lends itself to an acquisition of information.

Learning is the creative act that takes place in the relationship between an event and understanding. To understand requires an interpretive act based in a risk-taking venture. As we interpret a text, we also are assimilated into a new tradition, changing our history and ourselves. As such, interpretation is not a methodological act, but rather a transformative act. Hermeneutics and learning are inseparable. As part of their dissertation, my doctoral students write on what took place in their own lives during the research process. Such writing is extensively derived from the personal log they maintain during the research project. Whereas they were "always already" in a tradition, they see themselves during and after the research project living within a different horizon than before the research, now understanding what was previously alien. In learning to risk their previously held prejudices and come to new understandings along with others, they open up the possibilities for different ways to collaboratively address some of the critical problems we face in society today. The risk and the personal responsibility engendered in participatory hermeneutic research confirm the essential tension in our inquiry between the society we live in and the one we could create.

APPENDIXES

Appendix A:
Entree to Nepal
Jo Williams

My original plan was to read about Nepal, gain permission from the appropriate Nepalese officials to study there, prepare for research, leave the United States, carry out my research, and return to write it up. This plan was followed for the most part. Where it deviated was in receiving permission to carry out my research. Below I tell you about my experience in gaining entree for my research project (Williams, 1990) on the role of ritual in changes in the family, community and economy in Nepal.

In 1986, I began pursuing information about Nepal and was only able to locate one library, at the University of California at Berkeley, within the campus library system which had information about Middle Asia. I began finding limited information about Nepal at this University of California library. At this time, I met a gentleman from Nepal who advised me to write to Tribhuvan University for entrance, which I did in early 1987. After several letters, I received two letters of response, but no commitment; the gentleman from Nepal advised me to "just go," so I did.

Upon arrival in Kathmandu, Nepal, in October 1987, I spent my first night with two American women whom I had met on the plane en route from Bangkok. Early the next morning I set out to find the well-known Kathmandu Guest House where Dr. Donald Messerschmidt had stayed upon his arrival in Kathmandu. We spoke on the telephone, and Dr. Messerschmidt recommended the guest house to me as the opening to Nepal. It was a 30-minute walk to the guest house, and when I entered the paved driveway, I saw the stark but welcome site of what would be my future home. The front desk was busy with tourist requests, and I noticed then the gracious courtesy and attention that was extended to each person. I inquired about a room and was told that all rooms were filled, but, if I waited in the lobby, perhaps a room would become available. This, I came to learn, was the Asian way of getting things done; if I showed patience in waiting for hours on end for a request, I might get what I wanted. Shouting a demand, walking away, and returning three hours later to be shocked that no one had heard the request or completed the demand, was not the way to get things done.

Three hours later, a room was given to me. I was to pay two dollars a night for a fifth-floor walkup. I felt relief, comfort, and gratitude, and knew I was home. The ceiling of the room was water stained, a remainder from the rainy season, and a wooden-shuttered window opened to the majestic Himalayas, miles away. There was a wooden bed with a blanket sheet only, a table, a chair, and one wire hanger on the entrance door. However, it was a gift to have secured this room. The chair of my doctoral committee would arrive later, and we would joke about the two-dollar cell. Nevertheless, we both fell in love with the tiny kingdom of Nepal.

The bathroom down the hall was shared by all of the guests on the fifth floor. There was a 50 percent chance of the toilets working, so I learned to use the facilities at off-hours, early in the morning. All this would become familiar to me, including, later, my own space and time alone, a kind of time so cherished by Westerners, which would be the solace of aloneness in the two-dollar cell. Looking back on those first hours in Kathmandu, I remember that I opened my knapsack and wanted to hide in the wraps of it, but the better part of me said, "Get out there and keep going." Therefore, that is what I did.

The Kathmandu Guest House is located in the Thamel district of Kathmandu. Currently, this is where most Westerners who are not traveling with tour groups will stay during their visits to Nepal. From the entrance of the guest house out to the market, it becomes suddenly crowded with people shopping, workers carrying stock, and taxis carrying arriving guests to their lodgings. There are a few vehicles and hundreds of pedestrians crowding the streets. The following description reflects the district as it was a century ago. In 1877, Singh and Gunand (1966: 8) wrote: "The streets of Kathmandu are very narrow, mere lanes in fact. And the whole town is very dirty. . . . The streets, it is true, are swept in the center, and part of the filth is carried off by the sellers of manure; but to clean the drains would now be impossible without knocking down the entire city, as the whole ground is now saturated with filth."

Even today, the streets look much the same. Although the guest house driveway is cement, the streets (full of potholes) are made of dirt and are on average the width of a car and a half. Always the breathtaking view of the Himalayas dominates the crowded streets, the stench of garbage and feces, and the sounds of barking dogs.

The third summit conference of the heads of state of the South Asian Association for Regional Cooperation was about to be held in Kathmandu during the second month of my visit. I noticed that considerable attention was given to cleaning the streets. Many of the people commented that it was costing a lot to have this "face" cleaned up for the visiting dignitaries. The people I met said, "Wait and see; when the meeting is over, the streets will go back to being filthy again." However, this prediction would not appear to have been borne out. By the time of my second trip to Nepal in 1988, *Rising Nepal*, Kathmandu's English-language newspaper, carried such notices as "Let's Keep Our City Clean" on the banner. On the state-run television station there were daily instructional programs demonstrating the gathering and destruction of garbage, and the use of garbage cans and dumpsters. Later, I met a female factory owner who had been contracted to make these dumpsters. The people appeared to be cooperating in the cleanup effort. Not only the Halhul or Chami, noted as sweepers and cleaners in the caste system, but all people, regardless of rank or station, seemed more aware of community responsibility.

That first morning, I had just begun to walk through the tiny passageway from market to market when I heard a voice shouting "Miss Williams, Miss Williams!" At first I thought I had gone mad, imagining someone calling me on the other side of the planet, so I continued waking. Suddenly a young Nepalese man stood directly in front of me and said, "Miss Williams, is it you? Remember me? My name is Ghopal." Ghopal had been a student in San Francisco when I was Dean of Instruction, two years earlier, and we had been briefly acquainted. It was a most overpowering feeling to see him again, here, and I can only say that it felt like a spiritual reawakening. Ghopal would become my entree to Nepalese culture, ceremony, and family for my research project. He had been scheduled to return to the United States; however, because of an error on his visa, he had been detained in Nepal.

Later, Ghopal's brother, Kishor, would introduce the slogan "It takes two hands to clap." Now, Ghopal and I went together to the American Embassy to plead his case, and then to the Nepalese ministry, and within two weeks he was back at Golden Gate University in San Francisco to complete his senior undergraduate year. Kishor (a self-styled name for his real name, Durgolal) would become my brother, and make me welcome in his home and among the members of his family. He would also introduce me to a university instructor who would in turn introduce me to the university campus chief to facilitate my research request.

PERMISSION TO CONDUCT RESEARCH

During my first couple of weeks in Kathmandu, I would take a taxi (300 rupees, U.S. $15) to the Tribhuvan campus in Kirtiphur located outside the city. I was seeking an entree to list my research project according to the respected protocol in doing research in Nepal. After I knew better, I traveled by bus for 2 rupees, or 20 cents, per trip. The campus is located in sprawling countryside and is comprised of clay brick buildings. The area appeared to be almost deserted, with scarcely any landscaping. Cows and sheep were the only signs of life. This seemed odd to me then, as my experience of campus life was of beautiful landscaping and architecture, and the display of wealth everywhere.

I located the research center after walking up a stone path covered with overgrown grass and weeds and seeing a sign for it in English. I walked into a dimly lit hallway, still chilly from the cold night, and was greeted at the doorway by a person who spoke English and led me to a small office, where I met the research assistant. The assistant recognized my name, and asked what I was doing there. I answered that I had written several letters requesting that I be granted permission to live and conduct research in Nepal. I noticed the stacks of papers on the desk, which the assistant told me were all the research request files. I remembered the Nepalese gentleman back in the United States who had told me that I must simply get on a plane and arrive in Nepal, that this is the Nepalese way. You must just show up there, he instructed me, because the University has no budget for answering letters. Of course, this had not occurred to me. (The other side of this difficulty was convincing my doctoral committee that I indeed had entrance and permission to carry out my research in Nepal, so that I could proceed with the project.) The assistant was very kind and said that all of the request files were on the desk. I saw my university envelope immediately. We both smiled, and then opened the letter again. Due to unfavorably written research by non-national researchers, the government had recently changed its attitude of openness to researchers, and it appeared that I had arrived at a bad time. However, the university did interview me, and said I could begin the research and give them updated reports. I was instructed to let the university take the proposal. I would be told later whether I had permission to conduct research in Nepal. This was frustrating as well as mysterious to me, but those in charge seemed quite comfortable with the process. Indeed, I wondered how much it reflected the social processes in the community.

A basic book about education in Nepal had said that one should go to the Education Ministry. However, I knew that if I pursued the Education Ministry, the university would not grant me permission. If I returned home, I would never get permission. It was late December, though, and I still had no word. I appealed to Kishor for help, and in his calm way, he said, "Remember, it takes two hands to clap and in Nepal we have nothing to gain by granting you permission; we are poor people. Why don't you take the people to dinner at a fine restaurant and socialize, so they can know you and trust you, and we'll see what will happen." So on December 24, a table for eight was reserved for the campus chiefs and three instructors. I had wanted Kishor to come, but I was beginning to understand the social system. Knowing that his caste was number 22 on the caste chart, I knew that we would follow his plan. I would go; he would stay home. One week later I was granted permission to do the requested research.

MAKING CONTACT

I had now secured a home, had a family, and an entrance to the university. I even had a friend in the education field, because Kishor had introduced me to Naresh Mani Raya, a university instructor. However, I understood only a few words of Nepalese, which I had learned in the United States. I asked the Bhaktaphur campus chief who could be my teacher and he said, "The Americans need to go to the Peace Corps office, because they understand you best." Krishna Ram Khatri, the campus chief, had returned two years before from a U.S. university and understood such things.

I walked to the Peace Corps office to begin contact. Walking the #11 as called by the Nepalese, refers to our two legs, that is, the "11," became my way of life. The Western mind, perhaps, wants everything over and done with, but, in Nepal, I felt that I was using what in Manhattan would have been "time saved, " for we do not seem to know what to do with the time we so assiduously wish to save in the United States.

At the Peace Corps office, I heard about the man who was to become my teacher and friend, and, later, my brother. A former Peace Corps volunteer told me that Birendra Sherpa was the best teacher in all of Nepal. Despite my difficulties with learning languages, I would, if I persevered, be able to speak basic Nepali. I inquired about meeting Birendra Sherpa. I was told it would take one week for my request to be taken to him and returned with a response. It would take another week for us to set up a time and place to meet. This would be the pattern for arranging all of the research conversations I would carry out with teachers. I agreed to pay 100 rupees (U.S. $5) per lesson.

During the months we would spend together, Birendra Sherpa would become a dear friend, enabling me to know people from all sections and castes in Nepal.

DAILY LIFE

My first stay in Nepal was for three months. In one sense, this entire period was my entree to Nepal. Learning about the daily life in a country other than your own is part of one's entree. During my first stay in Nepal, my residence was the Kathmandu Guest House. This was a home base, where I could be reached by the people I met and conversed with and where friends could find me most evenings. Usually I would wake up at about 6:00 a.m., take a shower, and prepare for the day's meetings and conversations or go for walks to familiarize myself with various areas. There was a restaurant run by a Tibetan family alongside the guest house, and this was where I would usually have breakfast of coffee and oatmeal. Because there was no heat in the guest house, I was able to get up and out rather quickly each day. We had a telephone at the house, which provided a convenient means of scheduling meetings and conversations; most people, however, did not have telephones at their residence or business. I often saw telephones on the desks of administrators, but they would smile and tell me it was just for appearances and was not actually hooked up yet. In any case, it was always a challenge to get a telephone number, because there were no telephone books in Nepal at that time. Therefore, it was by chance that someone might have the telephone number of an official whom I needed to call. Usually, a business would have a telephone, and people would call and leave messages for various people.

Around 10:30 a.m., people would eat their midday lunch and then leave for work. Getting to work was an interesting process. Small, privately owned buses are the means of daily transportation, and they cost under one rupee for a ride to most areas in town. However, the few bench seats would invariably be filled by those people able to jump into the bus through its windows while it was stopped to unload passengers, so by the time one hopped up to the back door, it was too late to secure a seat. all the standing passengers would be crammed together, eyeball to eyeball.

I usually arrived for appointments at about noon, as this seemed to be the best time for interviews. At 2:00 p.m., the instructors would be finishing their day and hundreds of us would stand by the road, waiting for the sight of an oncoming bus. I used to plot how I would be able to climb up, grab the frame of a glassless bus window, and throw myself in. Much of people's energy was expended daily simply trying to get to and from their destination. The buses stopped running at nightfall, 7:00 p.m. in the summer and about 4:30 p.m. during the winter when the sun disappeared behind the mountains. Taxis were almost nowhere to be found after 8:30 p.m., and were only practical to travel to the airport; for shorter distances, one might be refused or quoted an extremely high fare. Taxi drivers also would refuse a Nepali passenger in favor of a Westerner.

Usually everyone went to the markets after work and brought home freshly harvested vegetables. Then the women would begin cooking. They served the men first and ate last. Meals usually consisted of tea, served first, and then rice and a vegetable. When I was invited into Nepali homes, I would sit cross-legged on the floor, usually on a woven straw mat over a clay floor, to be served the meal. The youngest child of the household would bring water in a copper cup, along with a copper bowl. I would hold my right hand over the bowl while the child poured water over it to wash off pollution. I ate with that hand, grasping the rice in a spoonlike manner, cupping my fingers around the rice, bringing them together, and putting the rice in my mouth. This tactile experience is one I miss with all the utensils we use at home.

During the day, I had to be aware that if I traveled after tea, I might have to use the side of the roadway with everyone else. Usually my host would offer me an area of land used for this purpose. Tea was offered in every household I entered, a most beautiful experience shared by the Nepalese people.

Birendra Sherpa took me to any destination he thought was necessary in order for me to know Nepal. The kindness I encountered throughout my travels took away most feelings of the loss of Western conveniences, such as running water, heat, or telephones. On many occasions, I would stay for one or more nights with a family. Birendra Sherpa was fond of his country and was pleased I was staying more than the usual three-week period for tourists. This time enabled mew to hear many stories from every person I met, about family, the importance of tradition, and the hunger for education and new information. Many wanted to hear about my life and family in the United States. We would walk to each person's school, where I would hear the history of how the school began, and listen to the person's ideas about education.

I found my participants in a variety of ways and in a variety of places. Naresh Mani Ray, Birendra Sherpa, Kishor D.L. Khadgi, and May Singh

Karki were the first people whom I met early on during my stay in Nepal
and who then introduced me to many of my research participants. I also
met people on my own in restaurants, on the streets, in homes, and in
shops. Other people heard about me and came to tell their story.

Since my initial research project, I have been back to Nepal twice. I am
sure I will return several more times — at least this is my plan. The stories I heard, the story I wrote, and the stories yet to come are now an
important part of me. Had the entree been conventional and had I received
permission with everything arranged for beforehand, I doubt that I would
have learned as much as I did about Nepal and my capacity for adventure
and new understandings. My Nepali entree was more than entering a different country, it was an unfolding of a living text that still is a dynamic
part of my life.

Appendix B:
Understanding Economic Development in Thailand through an Analysis of Play in a Research Conversation

Mary Abascal-Hildebrand

This analysis demonstrates the implications and possibilities that participatory research in a critical hermeneutic tradition can generate for understanding how future economic development in Thailand might take place. Using this approach, researchers, community developers, policymakers, and other government leaders can conceive of development issues overall. Further, its use is seen as a way for everyone involved to understand a particular context better so that all development participants can reap benefits through reclaiming a sense of community. There are complex influences on industrialization and on the policies that generate development; critical hermeneutic theory is seen as a way to interpret more of these complex influences than is possible when only attending to structural accounts of development.

A practical advantage is that, although developers can never fully understand the biases of their own thinking, they can become more aware of them through critical analysis. Writing about the limits of our knowing, in terms of Gadamer's hermeneutics, Weinsheimer (1985: 182) says, "There is always a remainder, an excess of what we are beyond what we know of ourselves, that makes self-consciousness incomplete." Gadamer (1976) also writes about biases; he says that they represent our opportunities to learn more during our conversations and that biases are our openness to the world. Hence, research participants can become more aware of their biases through conversations and critical analysis and use those stances to change their horizons.

The experiences portrayed in this analysis reveal why it is important to understand development from a contextual perspective. In the case of Thailand, it is necessary to view the interrelatedness of several themes, that is, political contexts, development approaches, and the philosophical view that undergirds such approaches. These themes gave the research conversation the direction, and provided the possibility, of play. Further, these themes provided a subject matter that stood in front of the conversation and served as a guide. Discussion of one theme prompted discussion of another, with frequent cross-references.

This conversation, during the course of two hours in an afternoon, took place between me and Mrs. Issariyaporn Chulajarta, a diplomat with the Thai Consulate in Los Angeles. To establish a context for our conversation, I began by talking briefly about what I had learned during my two recent visits to Thailand. I then asked her what she believes undergirds the relative long-term stability enjoyed in Thailand. This was the only planned question I asked, as all the other questions generated from our conversation. Gadamer (1976: 17) writes, "Genuine speaking, which has something to say and hence does not give prearranged signals, but rather seeks words through which one reaches the other person, is the universal human task."

Mrs. Chulajarta described Thailand as having a democratic government and noted that its stability comes from representing the needs of its people. She also noted its more successful development efforts come from carefully attending to what the people need by talking to them and not just assuming for them what they need. I told her that I knew that the Thai King promotes this approach to economic development. She explained, "He always goes to the remote areas to see the people, to ask about their needs, their living conditions, to see for himself." She elaborated, "He has formulated the Royal projects on the needs of the people, and the projects have worked because he has provided the basic needs."

In responding to my questions about the type and scope of Thai development, Mrs. Chulajarta noted that the government is developing projects along the seaboards and in the rural areas. I told her I knew about the Thai interest in developing feeder economies and the related issue of rural migration and its associated poverty problems. Her explanation added to what I had known, in a spiral of what I was coming to know: "The income gap and the unemployment problems are major concerns in Thailand. We are developing projects in the rural parts of the country to draw people to such sites."

When I asked what might draw the people to the rural projects, she talked about it in terms of resource distribution, "We have various industries started there and now all the raw materials for those do not come to be processed in Bangkok, but are processed in these rural areas." I contended that a community needs persons who can make a variety of contributions, and asked how those who were skilled were encouraged to move to the rural areas. Mrs. Chulajarta acknowledged my comment, noting that Thais were encouraged with employment possibilities, and Thailand is "looking for more engineers, and hopes Thai engineers working abroad would return to Thailand. We have work for them."

Concerning the philosophy that undergirds education, I noted that U.S. education typically focuses on education as a product, and that, although U.S. policymakers are very concerned with certain aspects of educational development, such as test scores, many U.S. students drop out before they finish secondary education. Contrasting this, I described Khit Pen, as I understood it — the Thai term for education as a lifelong process, not a product, for promoting both individual and community well-being in everyday life. I explained I understood that this emphasis on process guided informal educational programs, especially in rural areas. She was unfamiliar with Khit Pen specifically, saying, "I did not know about that philosophy," but she observed, pointing out the play in our conversation, "You seem to be quite familiar with our educational system."

Mrs. Chulajarta noted that the government was making changes in courses of study "because some courses were just not practical." She explained the education ministry "was adding courses so that, for example, students from the rural areas can use their knowledge to learn mathematics to learn more how to grow food instead of sticking only to mathematical drill." She elaborated, "so education will help the people develop their economy, subject to whatever resources are available to them." I asked how the educational and economic sectors communicate. I told her I was concerned about how any democratic, developing country could both promote its economy at the same time it safeguards education against undue economic influence.

Mrs. Chulajarta responded to the emerging flow in our conversation when she emphasized, "We want to put our economic development in more practical terms, more reality . . . to solve the city problems, the poverty problems, those in the rural areas." She explained how it may seem to others that Thailand has few problems and instead benefits from its fast-moving economy. She contrasted, "You have been there [Thailand] so you know. We have serious problems. Looking at the rapid

growth, we might say the economy grows a lot. We still have the problem
of income distribution, as well as poverty."

She explained the Thai emphasis on basic needs, "We concentrate on
raising the standard of living, not so much on the growth rate [of some
economic sectors]. It has to be growth with stability." She continued,
"according to the needs of the people in that community," elaborating, "it
doesn't have to be the same all over the country." This confirmed my
assumption that she referred to individuals as well as to local communities when she talked about basic needs. Then she added:

That makes me think of an important point: the problem we are facing in our economic development is that it seems like the government just speaks to the people.
But the people have to realize their needs themselves. The government cannot tell
them, "you have to have this housing, you have to have this sanitation, you have
to have a certain type of whatever." It doesn't work. People have to voice their
needs. That's the way we have to incorporate. If we just provide things, it's useless. The people have to want it also.

I gave Mrs. Chulajarta my view: "I think the key to our success in solving human problems is to find out what people believe they need" and the
play linked that to what she had just noted, "you see that this is still a need
in your country." She said, "Yes, looking at the past performance, I would
say so." I asked her what she thought would be needed so that the people
would have more voice. She played back, "To urge them to be more cooperative?" I returned, "Yes, to talk more about what they need, as you said."
Reflecting, she responded: "I am thinking about one of the things that you
mentioned earlier, when I was talking about certain projects for certain
areas. One of the things we need, because if we just provide for them what
we think is good, and it might not be good. They might consider they do
not need all those things, that they can live happily without them. We have
to try at different levels. We have to accept that ideas that are too recent
may be a problem."

She follows the play our conversation generates as it continues: she
says, "when I think about this I think about the aid from developed countries like Japan." As an example, she noted that the Thais shared many
projects with the Japanese government. She explained the Thai government was criticized by many of the people for projects that seemed to be
attempts to publicize Japan, such as the cultural projects or cultural centers (these centers are mainly visitors' attractions, with park-like com-
mercial overtones). She explained the paradox they create, "The cultural
projects are not productive. The Japanese want to publicize their work.

We consider that these sorts of projects are not worthwhile for us." She added, "We have more poverty projects that are needed, but Japan does not accept our priorities because they just want to provide whatever they want. That is a problem because we are the recipient country."

Following the movement of the conversation, I added, "that must have created a special kind of international relations challenge." She answered, "Yes, we couldn't do much. She talked about her role: "I used to have meetings [where] we debated quite a lot [and] tried to submit a three-year plan as guidance to solve the poverty problems" because "we need to solve these more than we need a cultural center." I asked, "Because they are more for show?" She answered, "Yes, that is the problem."

I told Mrs. Chulajarta about the Japanese-built hospital I had seen in Katmandu that was being finished to replace an older one still in use. (Projects sponsored by other governments also were prominent in the city so that this project was not unusual.) I also told her that the Australians were building a new airport terminal, the People's Republic of China built the ring road around the city, the Germans provided the funds to restore the ancient city, Baktopar, and the Koreans built the lighting system throughout Katmandu.

I explained that while I was in Nepal, I learned that the country's only children's orthopedic hospital (a small building that looks more like a small clinic than a hospital) depends on donations from trekkers to outfit its outpatient-care staff for travel to remote regions. I added that the day I visited most of the hospitalized children were from remote areas and were in crisis because their conditions had advanced while they were living in regions where medical care was nonexistent. I told her I thought that this health care need was being overlooked. The movement continued in the conversation as she responded: "Exactly, that is like the experience we have with Japan. We had a conversation with the Japanese government regarding something similar to this; they wanted to subsidize the education program for steel workers or certain other industries they feel [would] be an advantage for them."

Adding another example, she said a perplexing aspect of bilateral projects is that other countries will provide "the equipment, but not the technology so the workers know how to operate the equipment; we had this experience with textile machines." Then I added, "Or how to repair it." She responded, "Yes, no technology transfer—then we are in the situation that we have to buy more [machines] from them." We talked about what is needed for people to be able to talk together and listen more carefully to one another, and whether some are better at communication. Mrs. Chulajarta offered: "It's my personal feeling that as women we still have an advantage, we are more patient, we are more understanding, and we are more willing to listen to others' opinions — we don't have to agree with anyone about everything, but we are more willing to listen to them. People have to have attitudes towards women that encourage this. Here [United States] there a lot of things that are just so different from my culture, from my understandings."

I prompted another spiral in the conversation, "What do you think it would take in your culture to develop more of an attitude towards conversation as a way to solve problems?" The play that resulted prompted her to note that it might be best considered within the Thai cultural traditions, "our way of living, especially our religion. That's why we understand people, we have feelings towards others, we consider others' feelings." She said she was trying to understand U.S. ideas, but that it was complex, and it seemed that many Americans were concerned only about themselves. Her acknowledgment of her own thinking is an example of how play led her to comment that when people are too selfless, they may not want to improve their lives and "that might not make it good for economic development for people to be satisfied only with what they have — that would be a misapplication of the concept." She contrasted, "then they might be too satisfied, and not interested in helping develop the country, or solve the problems of the country; there needs to be a balance."

Continuing in this mode, I told her that I had read that Buddhist leaders were concerned that the Thai people were becoming too occupied with economic development in the form of competition and greed and were disregarding the needs of the people and of the environment. They were concerned that the Thai spirit would be lost in the fervor of economic development. She contended that for the best economic development "people need to be more positive in their education, in their careers, in everything." I asked what she thought was needed to avoid selfishness, yet at the same time encourage people to moderate being too selfless. She said she thought the Thais ought to "pay attention to the teachings of the Buddha by focusing on the way to live so economic development will be better for a rapidly growing society."

This to and fro movement enabled her to continue to acknowledge problems that can emerge when developers only consider the growth rate, "I think that they should focus on income distribution and poverty problems because they are more urgent than the [growth] rate; they are the indications of the well-being of the people." I asked Mrs. Chulajarta what she wanted most from those with whom she works here in the United States. She said she wants others to keep her well informed so she can know how to respond, but most importantly: "what I really need is their cooperation. I have to be aware of the constraints I have here [in the United States]. I don't have enough staff; we need consideration [from those in the United States] to be able to continue what we have done." I asked her which country was Thailand's best ally, and she responded that the United States was, but that its "actions speak louder than words." She noted that to be a more effective ally, U.S. policymakers need to know more about Thailand and realize how trade barriers affect Thailand's economy. She acknowledged me, saying "You have gone already, you have seen the poverty. We still need assistance."

I moved the spiral higher as I explained that because politicians in the United States respond to diverse constituencies, they often appear to neglect international issues; I asked her how politics affect deliberations in Thailand. She returned within this spiral as she said that she thought the politics were affected by the religious philosophy and the Thai traditions. I asked her if she believed Thais were able to plan long-term more readily than were Americans, saying, "There are those who say that Americans have more difficulty with working with others in international development because they look to the short-term." Disagreeing, she noted a particular irony: "I have a contrary view. It's one thing to have a long-term view if you can implement it. It's worthless if you can't implement it. I notice here [in the United States] that there is such good organization that people can get accomplished what they want to. It's hard to control all the parts in a long-term plan. It's hard to predict the problems."

She contrasted, "a short-term view might be more creative — to be able to dispense with an unworkable plan and change to one that is more workable."

Moving the play to an ever higher, or perhaps more abstract or general altitude, I asked her whether Thailand's participation in ASEAN (Association of Southeast Asian Nations) was helpful to the nation. She pointed out she thought ASEAN is more political now than it is action-oriented, especially because of the political conditions in Vietnam. She described the benefit in more direct communication with governments in the throes of political change, saying that such communication with Vietnam had brought major benefits to Indochina. Mrs. Chulajarta noted that Thailand's political and economic success belies the domino theory because its democratic government and trading policies support its efforts to strengthen the entire Southeast Asian community.

In this conversation, three themes were interrelated: Thailand's position in Southeast Asia, its development needs, and the influence of its philosophy and traditions on development. Further, my historical horizons and those of Mrs. Chulajarta's were interpreted by each of us so that the other could continue to participate in the conversation, and indeed question and interpret our own and one another's participation in the conversation.

Pointing to the play and spiraling introduces the reader to the possibilities for deeper understanding through critical hermeneutic analysis; the reader can understand how our conversation enabled us to see things differently than we did before we talked together because we could translate and interpret for one another. Gadamer (1988: 346) explains, "Thus the linguistic process by means of which a conversation in two different languages (mine as researcher, hers as economist) is made possible through translation is especially informative."

ANALYSIS OF PLAY AND THAI DEVELOPMENT

As we opened our conversation, we talked about the stability of Thailand in terms of the way the government considers "the needs of the people." Then we talked about the type and scope of development projects and followed that with conversation about concerns for the migration out of the rural areas and how projects were encouraging rural development. When I noted what I understood about the Khit Pen process, Mrs. Chulajarta indicated that she had been unaware of this process until I described it. This is an example of how conversation can enable us to rethink what we know; talk of Khit Pen enabled a fusion of horizons for her. Further, this fusion, or new way of thinking, prompted her to think about the changes in curriculum in Khit Pen terms, as she stipulated it was more practical and "will help the people develop their economy subject to whatever resources are available to them."

An example of the far-reaching nature of fusion is that much later I discovered that Khit Pen is a contemporary creation of curriculum developers working on a informal education project. A particular group of developers wanted to relate the project with Thai perspectives on community life. For this purpose, they created the Khit Pen process. In first hearing of it, I had assumed that it had a historical dimension. Therefore, later it was clearer to me why Mrs. Chulajarta was less likely than I had earlier expected to have known about Khit Pen. I then experienced another fusion of horizons at that point. My discovery of the invention of Khit Pen developed in a conversation I had with a university professor of educational philosophy, Terry Walker, from Indiana State University, as we spoke informally at a professional conference. I had heard that he had worked in Thailand, and our conversation led to my question about Khit Pen and his explanation about its origin.

The sense of play we felt in the conversation encouraged us to talk more about economic and educational sectors and to examine how they were communicating with one another. With this she could respond: they need to "put our economic development in more practical terms according to the needs of the people in that community. It doesn't have to be the same all over the country."

She stayed with this point, although she took it to greater altitudes in a spiral, as she replied to my question about whether developers actually had conversations with the people in communities. She stated, "That makes me think of an important point. The problem we are facing in our economic development is that it seems that the government just speaks to the people. But the people have to realize their needs themselves." She returns in the spiral, "People have to voice their needs. If we just provide, it's useless. The people have to want it also." Here Mrs. Chulajarta illustrates another altitude in her thinking about the needs of the people: she reflects that not only must the needs be considered in local terms, but the people must "realize their needs themselves, voice their needs and want it also." Her own analysis is apparent, as she engages in the conversation: she now begins to speak about the ways in which developers must consider the local needs — by considering peoples' priorities. Hence, her thinking, and the conversation, reached new altitudes as we talked together.

Her responses illustrate directly my participation in the conversation, not only my questions but also my responses generated her thinking within these new altitudes. As we examine this, we can see how she creates another spiral as she reaches a new point in her thinking: "I think one of the things you mentioned earlier when I was talking about certain projects for certain areas — that one of the things we need (reflective pause) — we just provide for them." We can see the play, "it might not be good. They might consider they do not need all those things. We have to try different levels, accept [what] may be a problem for them."

I interpret her remarks as saying developers must consider the local needs of the people by talking with them. They also must be aware that what they suggest and how people respond to their suggestions may need to be considered in terms of "different levels" so that persons in communities can actually commit to development projects in practical terms and in view of local priorities. She suggests that development must be construed in terms of how development projects relate to one another, from the community's perspective, "they might consider they do not need all those things."

The conversational to and fro in which we engaged over the suitability of some bilateral development projects — in particular those about

Japan's participation — prompted a fusion of my horizons: I had not thought earlier of this kind of development project as creating a paradox for the recipient country. I had seen many such projects in Thailand and Nepal. I had originally thought that the new Japanese-built hospital in Katmandu would solve the problems I had seen so clearly when I visited the children's orthopedic hospital. (Just weeks before my visit the hospital installed its first mechanized laundry equipment. Prior to that, staff had only been able to stomp-wash all bedding, bandages, and clothing and were still forced to rewash surgical gloves as an economic measure.) Hearing Mrs. Chulajarta's comments about bold projects that did not always meet actual needs made me rethink my earlier estimation of the hospital, and I commented that a different approach, one that considered satellite health care projects, might serve Nepalese needs better.

I had not thought about the bilateral projects in Nepal in the terms Mrs. Chulajarta introduced to me because I had been overwhelmed by the need in Nepal for development. I, too, had understood development in terms similar to those of the Japanese or the Nepalese — not in these newer terms. Through the experiences we both brought to the conversation and through the play we allowed in our conversation, we were able to promote this fusion of horizons that enabled me to understand development problems in new and different terms. We continued this spiral as we interpreted one another within our conversation.

This conversation helped bring into each of our thinking new horizons about development; that is, understandings that include the needs of the people in terms of Thailand's internal stability, curriculum change in schools, developers' responsibilities in looking at local needs, bilateral projects that present dilemmas for Thailand as a recipient country, and other international relations. By giving over to play, our conversation captured many of the major development issues for Thailand and demonstrates how conversation can open vistas much wider for us than is possible when we imagine that we can contemplate issues alone, or when we analyze data from structural accounts alone.

The very social conditions that shape conversation also are the very obstacles that prevent us from ever knowing directly, which in turn requires us to interpret using conversation. Hence, we must take the detour within interpretation both because of our ability to know directly and our ability to interpret. Ricoeur points out that a hermeneutic philosophy that aims at interpretation with question-posing demonstrates "the existence of an opaque subjectivity which expresses itself through the detour of countless mediations" (in Kearney, 1984: 32).

Because the questions we ask and the responses we give are our understandings, they cannot be separated from understanding the whole conversation. In talking with Mrs. Chulajarta, and in thinking about our conversation, I could not think of questions simply as tools that somehow uncovered only her thinking. I could not think of questions as if they could be linked only to the answers they might prompt, or the reverse. I had to think of both questions and answers as reflecting the thinking that emerged from the conversation as a whole, as part of all we both spoke to one another. I could only interpret what she said by virtue of interpreting individual questions and responses in the context of the whole conversation. Weinsheimer (1985: 210) writes, "every question implies several possible answers . . . it possesses not only a focus of statement or assertion but also a horizon of unasserted possibilities of meaning, which are the possibilities of interpretation that exceed what is stated in the text."

The analysis developed as I reflected on it and even as I was writing about it, but it was always *our* conversation I was analyzing: "speaking does not belong in the sphere of the 'I' but the sphere of the 'We'" (Gadamer 1976: 65). Applying this to Thailand's development issues, we can think about the way in which wider, ongoing assessment and reflection about the historical influences on development projects can more likely promote development that is responsive to changing thinking and to changing conditions. Ricoeur poses, "our future is guaranteed precisely by our ability to possess a narrative identity, to recollect the past in historical . . . form" (in Kearney, 1984: 28).

This analysis illustrates that we are less able to contemplate issues, particularly massive policy issues, in isolation. It is not just my analysis, for it emerged from our conversation. The fusion of horizons is not possible without the communication of the various actors. Thai development cannot proceed as if the parts of its development (economic, educational, social, and political) are considered as independent units. These various sectors must communicate with one another throughout, as must both sides of the private sector.

Just as my interpretation of the transcribed conversation creates a conversation with the reader, so too can development collaborators interpret their projects together. In other words, ongoing assessment and reflection are best conducted across sectors in a multisector collaboration within a society. This is beneficial because communication among persons in various sectors can enable them to see issues in ways they had not seen before. A fusion of new horizons is possible that promotes the interrelatedness of development projects.

The fusion has endless possibilities because it creates a new national memory that can continue to generate thinking: "To reword language is to rediscover what we are. What is lost in experience is often salvaged in language" (Ricoeur in Kearney 1984: 28). It makes it more likely that development projects will not end when the last component is put in place, or when the last outsider leaves. Rather, development can regenerate because the numerous multilevel conversations about its various activities can continue. It can continue to influence the thinking that generates new projects and new views about Thai politics and economics.

Social and economic development is difficult and complex to understand. However, this is actually an advantage because when we find something difficult to understand we can become more aware of the conditions we need for clarity (Gadamer 1975: 346). A new political development, such as a revolt against the military or government, can actually serve us in reinterpreting our ideas about Thai social and economic life. It becomes even more obvious why Thailand will not be able to embrace primarily technological solutions or merely structural and traditional empirical data and research processes to the exclusion of other approaches to understanding the complex development needs and visions for Thailand.

Bibliography

Achinstein, P. & S. Barker, eds.
  1969 The legacy of logical positivism/Studies in the philosophy of science. Baltimore, MD: Johns Hopkins University Press.
Ancel, D.
  1995 An interpretive approach to the mediation of culture and technology in the global workplace. Doctoral dissertation, University of San Francisco.
Beers, S.
  1980 Preface. *In* Autopoiesis and cognition. H. Maturana and F. Varela. Boston: D. Reidel Publishing Company.
Bellah, R., R. Madison, W. Sullivan, A. Swindler, & S. Tipon.
  1991 The good society. New York: Alfred A. Knopf.
  1985 Habits of the heart: Individualism and commitment in American life. Berkeley: University of California Press.
Berger, P. L. & T. Luckmann.
  1967 The social construction of reality. New York: Doubleday.
Bernstein, R. J.
  1983 Beyond objectivism and relativism. Philadelphia: University of Philadelphia Press.
  1976 The restructuring of social and political theory. Philadelphia: University of Pennsylvania Press.
Blamey, K.
  1995 From the ego to the self: A philosophical itinerary. *In* The philosophy of Paul Ricoeur. Lewis Edwin Hahn, ed. Chicago: Open Court.

Bohm, D.
   1980   Wholeness and the implicate order. London: Routledge & Kegan Paul.
Bowers, C. A.
   1987   Elements of a post-liberal theory of education. New York: Teachers
          College Press.
   1980   Curriculum as cultural reproduction: An examination of metaphor as a
          carrier of ideology. Teachers College Record 82(2).
Brown, L. D.
   1985   People-centered development and participatory research. Harvard
          Educational Review 55(1): 69–75.
Capra, F.
   1982   The turning point: Science, society, and the rising culture. New York:
          Bantam Books.
Chaney, R.
   1983   Evolution, human evaluation and self-overcoming. Paper delivered to
          the American Anthropological Association. Chicago, November 17.
   1978   Structure, realities and blindspots. American Anthropologist 80:
          589–596.
   1975   On epistemological presuppositions and the rules of the game. Current
          Anthropology 16, 641–642.
   1974   Anthropologies and histories, and philosophies of scientific inquiry. *In*
          Studies in cultural diffusion, Vol. 1. James Schaefer, ed. HRAF 1 ex,
          W6-002, Cross - Cultural Research Studies. New Haven: Human Rela-
          tions Area Files, Inc.
De Pree, M.
   1990   Leadership is an art. New York: Bantam Doubleday Dell Publishing
          Group.
Ebeling, G.
   1961   The nature of faith. London: Collins.
Edelman, M.
   1988   Political language and political reality. *In* Constructing the Political
          Spectacle. Chicago: University of Chicago Press.
   1977   Political language: Words that succeed and politics that fail. New
          York: Academic Press.
Eisner, E. & A. Peshkin, eds.
   1990   Qualitative inquiry in education/The continuing debate. New York:
          Teachers College.
Ermarth, M.
   1978   Wilhelm Dilthey: The critique of historical reason. Chicago: Universi-
          ty of Chicago Press.
Everhart, R.
   1979   Ethnography and educational policy: Love and marriage or strange
          bedfellows. *In* Anthropology and educational administration.

R. Barnhardt, J. Chilcott, and H. Wolcott, eds. Tuscon, AZ: Impressora Sahuaro.

Feigl, H.
1970 The "orthodox" view of theories. *In* Analysis of Theories and Methods of Physics and Psychology. M. Radner and S. Winokur, eds. Minneapolis: Free Press.

Foster, W.
1986 Paradigms and promises. New York: Prometheus Books.

Freire, P.
1985 The politics of education: Culture, power, and liberation. South Hadley, MA: Bergin and Garvey Publishers.
1973 Education for critical consciousness. New York: Seabury Press.

Fuchs, E.
1964 Studies of the historical Jesus. London: S.C.M.

Gadamer, H.
1988 Truth and method. New York: The Crossroad Publishing Company, (Original 1965, 1975 English.)
1976 Philosophical hermeneutics. D. Linge, trans. and ed. Berkeley: University of California Press.

Geertz, C.
1983 Local knowledge: Further essays in interpretive anthropology. New York: Basic Books, Inc.
1980 Blurred genres: The refiguration of social thought. American Scholar 49(2): 165–179.
1973 Thick description: Toward an interpretive theory of culture. *In* Interpretation of cultures. New York: Basic Books, Inc.

Giddens, A.
1976 New rules of sociological method: A positive critique of interpretive sociological method. London: Hutchinson.

Giroux, H. & D. Purpel.
1983 The hidden curriculum and moral education: Deception or discovery? Berkeley: McCutchan Publishing Corporation.

Gonzales, Ma. C. T.
1991 A political hermeneutic of curriculum policy-making at the national level in the Philippines. Doctoral dissertation, University of San Francisco.

Gould, S. J.
1982 Punctuated equilibrium: A different way of seeing. New Scientist 94 (April 15): 137–141.

Grundy, S.
1987 Curriculum: Product or praxis. New York: The Falmer Press.

Habermas, J.
1996 Between facts and norms: Contributions to a discourse theory of law and democracy. W. Rehg, trans. Cambridge: The MIT Press.

1989   The theory of communicative action: Lifeworld and system, a critique
        of functionalist reason, Vol. 2. Boston: Beacon Press. (Original 1981.)

1984   The theory of communicative action: Reason and the rationalization of
        society, Vol. 1. Boston: Beacon Press. (Original 1981.)

1982   A reply to my critics. *In* Habermas: Critical debates. J. B. Thompson
        and D. Held, eds. Cambridge, MA: The MIT Press.

1979   Communication and the evolution of society. Boston: Beacon Press.

1973   Legitimation crisis. Boston: Beacon Press.

1973a   Theory and practice. Boston: Beacon Press.

1971   Knowledge and human interest. Boston: Beacon Press.

1970   Toward a rational society. Boston: Beacon Press.

Hanson, N. R.

1969   Perception and discovery: An introduction to scientific inquiry. W. C.
        Humphreys, ed. San Francisco: Freeman, Cooper & Company.

Heidegger, M.

1977   The question concerning technology and other essays. New York:
        Harper Torchbooks.

1971   On the way to language. New York: Harper & Row Publishers.

1962   Being and time. New York: Harper & Row. (Seventh edition, original
        1927.)

1959   An introduction to metaphysics. New Haven: Yale University Press.

Herda, E. A.

1997   Global economic convergence and emerging forms of social organiza-
        tion. Proceedings of World Multiconference on Systemics, Cybernet-
        ics and Informatics, International Institute of Informatics and Sys-
        temics. July 7–11, Caracas, Venezuela, 4: 30–37.

1997a   Organizational change and mimesis$_{1\,2\,3}$. Proceedings of Philosophy of
        Education. Far West Philosophy of Education Society. December 5–6.
        A. LeGrand Richards, ed., Jamison Noorlander, assoc. ed. Brigham
        Young University, Provo, Utah, pp. 59–65.

1990   A critical hermeneutic analysis of foreign language teaching: Implica-
        tions for teachers in the People's Republic of China. The CATESOL
        (California Teachers of English to Speakers of Other Languages) Jour-
        nal 3(1).

Herda, E. A. & D. Messerschmitt.

1991   From words to actions: Communication for business management.
        Manchester: Manchester University Press.

Humboldt, W. von.

1988   On the task of the historian. *In* The hermeneutic reader. K. Mueller-
        Villmer, ed. New York: Continuum. (Original proceedings of the
        Berlin Academy of Science, 1822).

Kearney, R.

1984   Dialogues with contemporary continental thinkers. Manchester: Uni-
        versity of Manchester Press.

Keiffer, C.
  1981   Doing dialogic retrospection: Approaching empowerment through participatory research. Paper presented to Society for Applied Anthropology. April 20–24. University of Edinburgh, Scotland.

Kraeder, L.
  1974   Beyond structuralism: The dialectics of diachronic and synchronic methods in the human sciences. *In* The unconscious in culture. I. Rossi, ed. New York: Button and Company.

Kuhn, T.
  1970   The structure of scientific revolutions. Chicago: University of Chicago Press.

Lakatos, I. & A. Musgrave.
  1970   Criticism and the growth of knowledge. London: Cambridge University Press.

Makkreel, R.
  1975   Dilthey: Philosopher of the human sciences. Princeton, NJ: Princeton University Press.

Mander, J.
  1991   In the absence of the sacred: The failure of technology and the survival of the Indian nations. San Francisco: Sierra Club Books.

Maturana, H.
  1980   Biology and cognition (original 1970). *In* Autopoiesis and cognition: The realization of the living. H. Maturana and F. Varela. Boston: D. Reidel Publishing Company.
  1978   Biology of language: The epistemology of reality. *In* Psychology and biology of language and thought: Essays in honor of Eric Lenneberg. G. A. Miller and E. Lenneberg, eds. New York: Academic Press.

Maturana, H. & F. Varela.
  1980   Autopoiesis and cognition. Boston: D. Reidel Publishing Company.

McCarthy, T.
  1982   The critical theory of Jurgen Habermas. Cambridge, MA: The MIT Press.

McLaren, P.
  1989   Life in schools: An introduction to critical pedagogy in the foundations of education. New York: Longman.

Mead, M.
  1977   Applied anthropology: The state of the art. *In* Perspectives on anthropology 1976. Anthony F. C. Wallace, ed. Washington, DC: American Anthropological Association.

Millar, R.
  1989   Doing science: Images of science in science education. London: The Falmer Press.

Mishler, E.
    1979   Meaning in context: Is there any kind? Harvard Education Review
            49(1): 1–19.
Nadeau, R.
    1991   Mind, machines and human consciousness. Chicago: Contemporary
            Books.
Nelson, C.
    1992   A critical hermeneutic approach to science education: Developing sci-
            entific praxis. Doctoral dissertation, University of San Francisco.
Palmer, R. E.
    1969   Hermeneutics, interpretation theory in Schleiermacher, Dilthey, Hei-
            degger, and Gadamer. Evanston: Northwestern University Press.
Percy, W.
    1958   Symbol, consciousness and intersubjectivity. Journal of Philosophy
            15: 631–641.
Phelps, L. W.
    1988   Composition as a human science: Contributions to a self-understand-
            ing of a discipline. New York: Oxford University Press.
Pitkin, H.
    1972   Wittgenstein and justice. Berkeley: University of California Press.
Poeggeler, O.
    1972   Heidegger, topology of being. In On Heidegger and language. J. Kock-
            elmans, ed. Evanston: Northwestern University Press.
Pribram, K. ed.
    1976   Central processing of sensory input. Cambridge, MA: The MIT Press.
    1974   The neurosciences. Cambridge, MA: The MIT Press.
Prigogine, I.
    1980   From being to becoming: Time and complexity in the physical sci-
            ences. San Francisco: W. H. Freeman and Co.
Prigogine, I. & I. Stengers.
    1984   Order out of chaos. New York: Bantam Books.
Radnitzky, G.
    1973   Contemporary schools of metascience. Chicago: Henry Regnery
            Company.
Ricoeur, P.
    1995   Reply to Mario Valdes. In The philosophy of Paul Ricoeur. Lewis
            Edwin Hahn, ed. Chicago: Open Court.
    1995a   Figuring the sacred: Religion, narrative, and imagination. Minneapo-
            lis: Fortress Press.
    1992   Oneself as another. Chicago: University of Chicago Press.
    1988   Time and narrative, Vol. III. Chicago: University of Chicago Press.
    1985   Time and narrative, Vol. II. Chicago: University of Chicago Press.
    1984   Time and narrative, Vol. I. Chicago: University of Chicago Press.

1982 Paul Ricoeur: Hermeneutics and the human sciences. John B. Thompson, ed. New York: Cambridge University Press. (Original English version 1981.)

1974 Existence and hermeneutics. *In* The conflict of interpretations. D. Ihde, ed. Evanston: Northwestern Press.

Schleiermacher, F.D.E.

1977 Hermeneutics: The handwritten manuscripts by F. D. E. Schleiermacher. Heinz Kimmerle, ed. James Duke and Jack Forstman, trans. Missoula, MT: Scholars Press (English trans. of the second German edition; Heidelberg: Carl Winter, 1974).

Searle, J. R.

1979 Expression and meaning. Cambridge: Cambridge University Press.

Sheldrake, R.

1982 A new science of life: The hypothesis of formative causation. Los Angeles: J. P. Tarcher.

Singh, M. S. & P. S. Gunand

1966 History of Nepal. Calcutta: Ranjan Gupta.

Theobald, R.

1981 Beyond despair: A policy guide to the communications era. Washington, DC: Seven Locks Press.

Thompson, J. B. & D. Held

1982 Habermas: Critical debates. Cambridge, MA: The MIT Press.

Toulmin, S.

1982 The return to cosmology: Postmodern science and the theology of nature. Berkeley: University of California Press.

Watson, L.

1980 Lifetide: The biology of consciousness. New York: Simon and Schuster.

Weinsheimer, J.

1985 Gadamer's hermeneutics: A reading of truth and method. New Haven: Yale University Press.

Williams, J.

1990 A critical analysis of community, education and socioeconomic change in Nepal. Doctoral dissertation, University of San Francisco.

Willner, D.

1980 For whom the bells toll: Anthropologists advising on public policy. American Anthropologist 82(1).

Winograd, T. & F. Flores.

1986 Understanding computers and cognition: A new foundation for design. Norwood, NJ: Ablex Publishing Corporation.

Zachlod, C.

1990 Theory and practice in the selection and education of U.S. managers for overseas assignments: A study in communicative competence and the organizational experience of overseas personnel. Doctoral dissertation, University of San Francisco.

Index

ABOUT THE AUTHOR

Ellen A. Herda directs the Pacific Leadership and International studies program in the Department of Organization and Leadership in the School of Education at the University of San Francisco.

ISBN 0-275-96105-2

90000>

EAN

9 780275 961053

HARDCOVER BAR CODE